SOCIAL EXISTENCE

Volume 141, Sage Library of Social Research

RECENT VOLUMES IN
SAGE LIBRARY OF SOCIAL RESEARCH

SOCIAL EXISTENCE

Metaphysics, Marxism, and
the Social Sciences

RICHARD QUINNEY

Volume 141
SAGE LIBRARY OF
SOCIAL RESEARCH

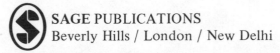
SAGE PUBLICATIONS
Beverly Hills / London / New Delhi

For information address:

SAGE Publications, Inc.
275 South Beverly Drive
Beverly Hills, California 90212

SAGE Publications India Pvt. Ltd. SAGE Publications Ltd
C-236 Defence Colony 28 Banner Street
New Delhi 110 024, India London EC1Y 8QE, England

Printed in the United States of America

Library of Congress Cataloging in Publication Data

Quinney, Richard.
Social existence.

(Sage library of social research ; v. 141)
Includes bibliographical references and index.
1. Sociology—Philosophy.   2. Sociology,
Knowledge of.   I. Title.   II. Series.
HM24.Q55 1982   301'.01   82-5903
ISBN 0-8039-0830-X   AACR2
ISBN 0-8039-0831-8 (pbk.)

FIRST PRINTING

To my daughters
Laura and Anne

Contents

We are travelling with tremendous speed toward a star in the
Milky Way. A great repose is visible on the face of the earth.
My heart's a little fast. Otherwise everything is fine.

—Bertolt Brecht, *The First Psalm*

Not till we are lost, in other words, not till we have lost the world,
do we begin to find ourselves, and realize where we are and the
infinite extent of our relations.

—Henry David Thoreau, *Walden*

It is not regret for the sunken Atlantides that animates us,
but hope for a re-creation of language. Beyond the desert of
criticism, we wish to be called again.

—Paul Ricoeur, *The Symbolism of Evil*

Some day you will be one of those who lived long ago.
The earth will remember you, just as it remembers the grass
and the forests.

—Pär Lagerkvist, *Evening Land*

Introduction

How are we to speak about that to which we attend? How are we to attend to what we cannot yet speak about? We are in a world given to us in all of our history, imagination, and collective experience. That world is continually becoming known to us. Being revealed—in historically specific form—is an order in the universe. There is a meaning in the world. Our struggle for social existence is a search for that meaning and an attempt at its fulfillment. The expectation that comes to us prophetically is for a worldly kingdom filled with unconditioned meaning. That we are beginning to regain a sense of original purpose and a way of understanding that purpose is the message of this discourse.

Social analysis has tried systematically to exclude the metaphysical from interpretation and understanding. Other concepts of reality—whether referring to an order of natural processes, the social structure, or the self—have been substituted in the consuming objective of finding first cause. When all these are abandoned there is still the human language within which we search for some order and meaning. Perhaps dialectically out of this latter search, out of hermeneutical understanding, we are starting to recognize the importance of speaking and interpreting. Through language and interpretation we begin to reconstruct the symbols that give meaning to our existence.

The task ahead, I am suggesting, is to create the symbols that will allow us as human social beings to find our place in the world again. The contemporary crisis is both material and symbolic; a social existence cannot be constructed without attending to both the conditions of material existence and the symbols for social and spiritual existence. Our hope is for a social existence filled with a meaning that relates to an order in the universe. Our immediate work is in the reconstruction of symbols in the struggle for social existence.

Throughout this discourse I draw from the symbolism of the prophetic Judeo-Christian tradition. This is the symbolism that has formed the basis of Western intellectual and spiritual existence. However, much of this symbolism has been rejected or suppressed in the contemporary academy and in everyday life, an alternative symbolism has not developed. This is the major crisis in our thought and in our lives. The traditional metaphysic, with the emphasis on the God-question, while addressing the essential problems of social existence, does not seem to be entirely appropriate for the contemporary sensibility. The two-world theory of reality—the earthly world opposed to the real world beyond—is in need of revision. There remains the need for a symbolism that gives depth to our existence. The answer is not to think and live without symbols, but to reconstruct a symbolic system that returns meaning to our existence.

Whatever the reconstructed metaphysic looks like, it will most certainly contain the element of that which we have known as religion. A metaphysic of social existence necessarily apprehends the historical in relation to the transhistorical, or, to use the traditional Judeo-Christian symbol, the temporal in terms of the eternal. The religious character of our existence is more than a figment of cultural creation. The religious is known culturally, but it also transcends culture in its purpose and meaning. A reconstructed metaphysic will undoubtedly unite what we traditionally have divided into the separate realms of the sacred and the secular. Holistically we live and have our being—our social being—in a reality that is at once finite and universal.

As social scientists (as we are called in this age), we give witness to the possibility of social existence. The tragic character of our project is the continuing disparity between our interpretive constructions and the knowledge and symbols that are necessary in the struggle for social existence. That there are moments when our efforts are appropriate is the hope and objective of critical reflection. We are in the long tradition of the world coming to know itself. The meaning of social existence is being revealed to us.

*   *   *

The contemporary development of the social sciences represents the culmination of a social and moral trend that has been accelerating for some time: the trend toward metaphysical skepticism and indifference. As a modern, advanced capitalist society has required an areligious and secular spirit to justify an economy of exploitation, a social science has developed to provide the symbols and explanations to support the further advancement of the social and economic order as well as to legitimize its present practices. Contemporary social science lacks the symbols that will allow us both to critically understand and to change the conditions of modern social existence.

The malaise in social theory, in particular, is increasingly being recognized. Contemporary theory is not, in fact, playing an active part in social science.[1] Although a dominant social theory prevails that is representative and supportive of the general crisis in the social and economic order, a dynamic and new theory—perhaps including a synthesis that draws from other traditions—has failed to develop. The functionalism versus conflict debate of the 1960s is no longer rel-

evant, and the forms of Marxist theory have yet to break
through the conservative and liberal resistance of the 1970s
and 1980s. The time seems especially to need a renewal in
social theory.

In the meantime, as part of the process of renewal, we seek
to grasp where we have been and where we might be going.
Our understanding is taking place primarily through the
notion of the *paradigm*. The recent studies of the history and
current status of social theory are organized around paradigmatic formations and shifts, drawing from Thomas S.
Kuhn's model of the scientific enterprise.[2] In a recent analysis of the use of the paradigm concept in sociology, however, it is shown that the critical meaning of the concept has
been misunderstood.[3] Particularly, there are three levels in
Kuhn's notion: (1) a broad level of unquestioned presuppositions, the *metaparadigm*, (2) a *disciplinary matrix* that represents the shared commitments of a discipline or a portion of
a discipline, and (3) the most concrete level, the *exemplar*,
which allows puzzle-solving to take place. The point is then
made that paradigms on the concrete level are likely impossible for sociology on a discipline-wide basis, but that concrete paradigms may be possible within the substantive areas
of research. This suggests that social theory of the "middle
range," or, more appropriately, of the "lower range," may be
developing within the substantive areas of sociology.

Yet, the nature of these social theories is bounded by the
most basic of theory, the general theory that is on the level
of the metaparadigm. When we speak of social theory of the
most general form, we are in the realm of *metaparadigmatic
theory*. All other theory is encapsulated by the larger framework of metaparadigmatic theory. It is this most general and
consuming level of social theory to which I am giving primary
attention.

I am arguing, moreover, that this most general and con-
sequential level of social theory—metaparadigmatic theory—is

also and necessarily in the realm of *metaphysics*. The meta-paradigmatic theory in social science makes us confront anew the metaphysics of social existence. To avoid the metaphysical question—the question of the reality of our existence as a whole—is to denature theory of its rightful claim and its essential quality. The renewal of social theory, I am contending, requires that we enter into the realm of the metaphysical. Without such consideration, social theory will most likely remain in its present state of malaise, failing to realize its potential in the understanding and the reconstruction of social existence.

* * *

For some time, then, we have been pursuing one kind of social theory. In spite of all the conceptual and problem-solving schemes, social theory is of a single character with only one general form. That theory is characterized by what can be called the *secularized metaparadigm*.

The secularized metaparadigm is, by conception, antimeta-physical—although such a stance is a metaphysic in its own right. Certainly the paradigm makes an explicit attempt to exclude questions traditionally incorporated into a metaphysical paradigm. Contemporary social theory thus systematically excludes questions about ultimate and transcendent concern, or about the reality of anything beyond the "natural" world. A meaning in the universe beyond the concrete facts and structures of daily life is not entertained in the secularized metaparadigm.

The clear alternative to the secularized metaparadigm is what can be termed simply the *sacred metaparadigm*. Here the primary, if not entire, focus is on the reality of the "other," or supernatural, world. Both the secularized and the sacred metaparadigms assume the traditional metaphysic of radical dualism, distinguishing between a natural world and a supernatural world. Each has made the decision as to which world is the real one.

With the secular version there is the sharp contrast between the reality of social life and the irrationality of spiritual and religious life. The radical dualism contained in the secularized metaparadigm reinforces that apparent contrast between a true realm of worldly existence and a fictitious realm of spiritual life, just as the sacred metaparadigm exalts a reality apart from social existence.

But the modern trend, usually ignored by social scientists, is the collapse of the metaphysical dualism (the material and natural world versus the nonmaterial and spiritual world). As Robert Bellah indicates, modern culture is being infused with a multiplicity of symbols that attempt to unite the realms of our existence.[4] In broadest terms we are reaching a point in cultural development that calls for a holistic metaphysic. To be created is a symbolic system that speaks to the wholeness of our existence.

For sociologists the problem is becoming that of integrating metaphysical, nonmaterial considerations into the analysis of social reality. A totally secular emphasis on the material world of social structure and everyday life evades the needs and trends in the larger culture. Certainly we cannot go back to the traditional sacred metaphysic, one that is "presociological."[5] Rather, we have to raise the questions of our total existence within the context of the modern ("postmodern") sensibility that is emerging.

The problem of the meaning of our being in the universe—the relation of our material and nonmaterial being in the social existence that we create and in which we have our whole being—is becoming the crucial problem of social inquiry in our time at the end of the twentieth century. The task is to construct a symbolism, in the form of social theory, for the emerging age, one that helps us as well to understand critically the contemporary condition.

What I am proposing, then, to begin this process, is the shift from the dominant (and sole) metaparadigm—the secularized metaparadigm—to a new metaparadigm. The latter I shall call the *holistic metaparadigm*, integrating the secular and sacred realms into a new, holistic paradigm and thus explicitly incorporating the metaphysical problem into social theory. This will be a form of thought that finds meaning in a social existence relating to the metaphysical questions of the universe.

* * *

Thus, the problem begins as an epistemological and hermeneutical question: How are we to speak again? How are we to develop an understanding of our social existence that allows us to be whole in the world? The approach I am developing concentrates on the meaning of social existence, drawing from some of the emerging notions in "postmodern" philosophical inquiry. What is needed is a paradigm change in the social sciences that will incorporate the problems excluded from the normal paradigms. We need to create a social existence that makes our being possible. We seek to become at one again with the world.

NOTES

1. See Norbert Wiley, "Recent Journal Sociology: The Substitution of Method for Theory," *Contemporary Sociology,* 8 (November 1979), pp. 793-799.

2. Thomas S. Kuhn, *The Structure of Scientific Revolutions,* 2nd ed. (Chicago: University of Chicago Press, 1970).

3. Douglas Lee Eckberg and Lester Hill, Jr., "The Paradigm Concept and Sociology: A Critical Review," *American Sociological Review,* 44 (December 1979), pp. 925-937.

4. Robert Bellah, *Beyond Belief: Essays on Religion in a Post-Traditional World* (New York: Harper & Row, 1970), pp. 20-50.

5. Graham C. Kinloch, *Sociological Theory: Its Development and Major Paradigms* (New York: McGraw-Hill, 1977), pp. 54-55.

1

The Search
for Meaning

Before heaven and earth
There was something nebulous
   silent isolated
   unchanging and alone
   eternal
   the Mother of All Things
I do not know its name
I call it Tao.[1]

In the beginning God created
The heavens and the earth
The earth was without form and void
   and darkness was upon the face of
   the deep
and the Spirit of God was moving
   over the face of the waters
And God said, "Let there be light"
and there was light.[2]

In the silence of the universe—the beauty to which every part is equally related—is our beginning. The silence of the uncreated world is already filled with the word: "In the beginning was the Word, and the Word was with God, and the Word was God" (John 1:1).

The Word Becomes Known

How does the word become known to us? What name do we give the word? In the naming we begin to apprehend the meaning of our lives in the universe.

To the word in the universe we humans have tended to give personal character. We speak anthropomorphically, not about *logos*, the word, the source beyond all being, but about "the word of God." In the Judeo-Christian tradition the word becomes the one God-being; more specifically, it is personified in the male-figure God.[3] The creation and the world thereof are thus made known to us in a unique image. Embodied in God, the word reveals to us a meaning in the universe and in our history.

In the Judeo-Christian grasp of the meaning, in the apprehension of infinite wisdom, "the Word became flesh and dwelt among us" (John 1:14). Our bodies, minds, and souls—all of our being—make concrete the word that is infinite and eternal. The human form is that through which the universe comes to know itself, the evolution of a cosmos of pure consciousness. The word comes to us in flesh, in time and space.

For us human beings, the word has become known, however mystically, through the practical medium of language, by speaking the word. St. Augustine in his treatise *On Christian Doctrine* makes the physical and spiritual connection:

> How did He come except that "the Word was made flesh, and dwelt among us"? It is as when we speak. In order that what we are thinking may reach the mind of the listener through the fleshy ears, that which we have in mind is expressed in words and is called speech. But our thought is not transformed into sounds; it remains entire in itself and assumes the form of words by means of which it may reach the ears without suffering any deterioration in itself. In the same way the Word of God was made flesh without change that He might dwell among us.[4]

The problem is that of speaking well, which is to say truthfully. Augustine continues: "But in all their utterances they should first of all seek to speak so that they may be understood, speaking in so far as they are able with such clarity that either he who does not understand is very slow or that the difficulty and subtlety lie not in the manner of speaking but in the things which we wish to explain and show, so that this is the reason why we are understood less, or more slowly."[5] It is not the eloquence of the speaking but the clarity of it that is important in representing the word. Good speaking of the word is also, and most important, a way of living. Making the word known is at the same time a form of life.

Hence, the word is made known to us through the word— in the context of our lives. But the gift of knowing the word has the double edge of not only the gaining of knowledge but also the loss of our origin in the totality of the universe. Our oneness with the cosmos has been shattered. In the Judeo-Christian imagery, this is the myth of the fall in the Garden of Eden. The human being in the eating of the forbidden fruit of self-consciousness has appropriated the origin that was once the secret of God. This is the moment when we moved from the origin in which only one thing is known— God—to knowledge about ourselves and other things as well. No longer can things be known only in God; now all things are mediated through human conscience and action. With the knowledge of good and evil we are no longer completely within the origin, the word. We know ourselves as something apart from God, no longer being purely of the word.

The human being has thus become estranged from the origin. The twentieth-century theologian Dietrich Bonhoeffer writes: "Instead of knowing himself solely in the reality of being chosen and loved by God, he must now know himself in the possibility of choosing and of being the origin of good and evil. He has become like God, but against God."[6] We have become to a considerable and practical extent our own God. Human beings now have the awesome task of under-standing the world, or as Søren Kierkegaard characterized it, of conducting ourselves in the terror of the universe. In our disunion with the world all things are in disunion, and our hope (our salvation and reconciliation) is in coming to know as fully as possible the word of God. We have been thrown into the terrifying responsibility of giving meaning to our lives and to human existence. The word is in the flesh; and in the flesh we regain, however approximately, our origin, our oneness in the universe.

As human beings we are knowers in the same language as the creator. God, in the Judeo-Christian religious tradition, created human beings in his own image: "So God created man in his own image, in the image of God he created him; male and female he created them" (Genesis 1:27). The knower is created in the image of the creator. Yet as Walter Benjamin writes:

All human language is only reflection of the word in name. Name is no closer to the word than knowledge to creation. The infinity of all human language always remains limited and analytical in nature in comparison to the absolutely unlimited and creative infinity of the divine word.[7]

In spite of the separation from the origin that necessarily takes place in the course of knowing, it is only in our knowing of the word that we reconstruct meaning in the world. Life is consciousness in the universe, the process of the universe knowing itself. The word becomes known ultimately.

Being in the World

In the meantime, what is it to be human, to be alive, to be human beings in the world, to die? And how is our social existence experienced in a time when the nature of our being is problematical? To be specific: What is the meaning of my life? What is the meaning and purpose of all life? How and why are our lives connected in the origin and expansion of the universe? Why is there something rather than nothing? To what do I appeal in my search for meaning? Why do I—why do we—seek a meaning to our lives and to the universe? And why are these matters so crucial to us at this time? These questions are for us of ultimate concern—at once religious, philosophical, and sociological.

To ask these questions is to place ourselves in an ancient and continuing stream of reflective thought. In the modern era, our reflective consciousness is shaped by existential and phenomenological thinking about "being-in-the-world." Our own quest necessarily begins with this body of thought—indeed, this thought represents a way of being in the world. But I shall attempt in my treatise on the meaning of social existence to integrate these assumptions when possible, or revise when necessary, into current and emerging ideas in various disciplines, going beyond particular fields of inquiry. The objective is the search for a meaning that we find in, and only through, our social existence. We are beings in a social world, finding meaning in and through that world. We construct and live a critical theory of social existence.

The meaning of our lives begins in an understanding of ourselves as *human beings*. Our being is not only made known in the process of thinking about our being, but in fact emerges and is realized in the course of the inquiry. Being, then, is a kind of existence that involves an understanding of being. This being that we are, which includes inquiry among the possibilities of being, is what Martin Heidegger formulates terminologically as *Dasein*.[8] In the phenomenological sense, being is concerned about its very being; being is a possibility in time that emerges in the process of thinking about our being. We are, as human beings with consciousness, continuously engaged in the struggle for our being. Our being is realized in the search for meaning.

That meaning—the search for meaning—is found in our
being-in-the-world. To be *in* the world means to dwell in and
to be at home there. The *world* signifies not a spatial realm
(earthly or heavenly), but the openness of Being.[9] The world
is that realm of consciousness and activity in which things
and events have meaning for us.

Homelessness is coming to be our destiny in the modern
age. We are without dwelling, without a home in the world,
when we cease to have meaning in our lives. We are without
home, surely, when we cease the search for meaning. We
regain our being when we return to the struggle for our being,
when we begin to search again. In that struggle—in the search
for meaning in our lives—we create the human structures
(social, economic, political, and religious) that make being
possible. We construct a world of meaning in everyday life. In
the structures of everyday life we then find the meaning of
our being.

The world is constructed and reproduced in our social
activity as human beings. The world is revealed to us, and we
are revealed to the world, through thought and action. We
think and act in the language that is granted unto us. Our
language, as Hans-Georg Gadamer presupposes, is our historical fate, the particular way being is revealed (and concealed) in our time.[10] The language of our social existence—
the language that reveals the word of our origin, however
historically unique that word may be—allows us to be human.
In the words and structure of our language, lived concretely
in social existence, we realize the possiblities of our ontological being.

Ontological Existence

Our being-in-the-world is shaped by the very nature of our
existence. Human being is fated, as Kierkegaard noted in his
discussion of "dread," to become conscious of itself.[11]

Moving beyond childhood innocence, we separate ourselves from our origin, becoming self-conscious of our ambiguous condition. With developing consciousness we naturally become anxious about our finite condition and about the choices we have within that finitude. Through our ontological anxiety we seek meaning for our mortal lives—faced certainly with death—in an infinite universe.

That we may become lost in the universe, even while alive, is a part of our human anxiety. The self may become lost; we may become alienated from our social existence; we may go mad in the process; we may no longer have any meaning in our lives. This is to fall from grace. In anxiety we fall and possibly regain our posture in the world again.

Between the fall and the salvation is the territory that includes nonbeing as well as being. Anxiety is felt most acutely in the apprehension of nothingness. Nonbeing is apprehended not only in the fear of a nothingness of death, but also in the threat of the meaninglessness of existence. In a modern version of the ontological problem of anxiety, "anxiety is the experience of Being affirming itself against Nonbeing."[12] The search for meaning, prompted by anxiety, is the denial of the nothingness of our being.

Because our being is ontologically in the process of realizing itself, nonbeing is ontologically as basic as being. Thus, as Paul Tillich argues, being has within itself nonbeing, and "anxiety is the state in which being is aware of its possible nonbeing."[13] The situation is existential, the awareness that nonbeing is a part of one's being, the recognition of one's finitude. Our finitude and our anxiety about it cannot be eliminated, because finitude belongs to existence itself. But our finitude is apprehended in the development of our being, with the finding of meaning in our lives. And that meaning is ultimately spiritual. Tillich writes:

The anxiety of meaninglessness is anxiety about the loss of an ultimate concern, of a meaning which gives mean-

ing to all meanings. This anxiety is aroused by the loss
of a spiritual center, of an answer, however symbolic
and indirect, to the question of the meaning of
existence.[14]

The search for meaning, whatever else it may be, is essentially
a spiritual search.

The spiritual search for meaning is necessary in order to
cope with the anxiety that is ontological to our being. Our
being is always incomplete; its possibility is always ahead of
us. Within the incompleteness of our lives is the fact of the
conditionality of everyday existence. Finally, as human
beings we seek to find our home in the world. The entire
process is what Heidegger calls care (Sorge).[15] It is ontological to our being that our existence is characterized by the
anxiety-filled need to become that which we are not, the
strain toward essence. Our essence is in the world with
others—in our social existence.

The conditions of our existence provide the setting for the
possibilities of creation and fulfillment. Within the Judeo-
Christian prophetic tradition of our culture—as represented in
both existential theology and Marxism—there is "the con-
fidence that what is is not utterly removed from what should
be; that in spite of the present lack of fulfillment, being is
moving in the direction of fulfillment."[16] The ontology of
being is that our social existence is moving in the direction of
that which is demanded.

In the symbolism of the prophetic tradition there are three
fundamental concepts that characterize the problem of existence and essence. Tillich writes:

First: *Esse qua esse bonum est.* This Latin phrase is a
basic dogma of Christianity. It means "Being as being is
good," or in the biblical mythological form: God saw
everything that he had created, and behold, it was good.

The second statement is the universal fall—fall meaning
the transition from this essential goodness into existential estrangement from oneself, which happens in every
living being and in every time. The third statement
refers to the possibility of salvation. We should remember that salvation is derived from *salvus* or *salus* in
Latin, which means "healed" or "whole," as opposed to
disruptiveness.[17]

These three considerations—goodness, estrangement, and the
possibility of something else—necessarily point to the fundamental nature of our contemporary condition.

It is in the contemporary historical situation under capitalism, as Karl Marx observed, that our essential being is
deprived.[18] The separation of existence and essence is the
tragic condition of human life in capitalist society. The
contemporary capitalist world is caught in what Tillich, going
beyond a materialist analysis of capitalism, calls a *sacred
void*, the human predicament on both a spiritual and a
sociopolitical level.[19] Among the vacuous characteristics of
present civilization are a mode of production that enslaves
workers, an analytic rationalism that saps the vital forces of
life and transforms everything (including human beings) into
an object of calculation and control, the loss of feeling for
the translucence of nature and the sense of history, the
demotion of our world to a mere environment, a secularized
humanism that cuts us off from our creative sources, the
demonic quality of the political state, and the hopelessness of
the future.

From the existential condition of capitalist society
emerges the possibility of a transformation that will allow us
to achieve the full potential of our being. Because the conditions under which we live in capitalist society divorce us from
our essential nature, transformation of the world becomes
necessary.[20] Capitalism is transformed into socialism. The

socialist demand is confirmed by our being: "The forces in the proletarian struggle, the revolt of primal humanity in the proletarian against the class situation, drive toward a socialist society. The promise of socialism grows out of the analysis of being itself."[21]

True social existence, therefore, is impossible under the conditions of capitalism; and true humanity can be achieved only in a protest against this estrangement. Not only must human physical existence be revitalized, but spiritual and social life also have to be restored. The ontology of being, in fact, moves us to inquire continually into the meaning of our social existence and to question the estrangement of this existence from our essential being. To understand the conditions of our existence is to engage simultaneously in the transformation of our lives and of the society in which we live.

In the transformation, in closing the separation between existence and essence, we create a reality in which our wholeness is more fully realized. Through human praxis the unity of subject and object, production and product, spirit and matter, becomes known. We become the subjects (the "movers of history") in the world we create. Thus, Karel Kosík observes, "The world of reality is not a secularized image of paradise, of a ready-made and timeless state, but is a process in which mankind and the individual *realize* their truth, i.e., humanize man."[22] The specifics of truth are not given and preordained, but are constructed in the process of searching for the unity of being in the world. Being essentially human is realized in the course of transforming our social existence.

A Question of Metaphysics

The development of capitalist existence represents the end of a social and moral trend that has been accelerating for some time: the trend toward religious skepticism and indifference. The advanced capitalist society has become the most secular society that the history of this world has known. Advanced capitalism is also advanced secularism. That developing capitalism and developing secularity have gone hand in hand is due to the internal demands of capitalism. An economy of exploitation requires an areligious spirit that legitimizes the further development of the economy as well as its present practices.

Writing in a Nazi prison in 1944 to a pastor friend, Bonhoeffer outlined the religious landscape of Western civilization. Soon to be executed by his persecutors for his role in the German Resistance, Bonhoeffer described in agonizing clarity the all but total secularization of culture. He wrote with pressing concern about the world's "great defection from God," indicating that the secular movement has reached a "certain completion," and that we have "learned to cope with all questions of importance without recourse to God as a working hypothesis."[23] In questions of science, art, and even ethics, the metaphysic of a supreme being or force is rarely considered anymore.

The drift toward secularism, as Bonhoeffer observed, represents the culmination of a movement that began in the Middle Ages. Its sources are many and complex. Certainly, the older, theistic conceptions could not understand—or be appropriate for—the intellectual, political, and economic developments of the subsequent centuries. And in our century, as the intellectual historian Franklin L. Baumer points out, the increasing belief in the relativity of history undermines a belief in any absolute notion of human existence: "History showed everything, law, morality, religion, and art, to be in ceaseless flux."[24] The postwar era has been characterized—intellectually and spiritually—by a belief in the relativity and transitoriness of all things. The malaise is both a product and a cause of the current tendency to reject or refuse to raise questions of ultimate concern. Whether an interest is lost in religious questions (remaining silent about such questions) or the mood is one of despair regarding the ultimate, our age is reaching the final stage in a long process of secularization.

The crisis of advanced capitalism is thus a crisis that is both material and spiritual. Materially, capitalism has reached a point at which it cannot advance economically or politically without altering the basic capitalist mode of production. The social problems created by capitalist production can no longer be solved within the framework of capitalism. And the capitalist state, once a political device for dealing with the economic contradictions of capitalism, is nearing the end of its ability to accommodate the problems of developing capitalism; the capitalist state itself is increasingly subject to contradictions and crises.

Spiritually, capitalism, once characterized by an unquestioning enthusiasm for acquisition and accumulation, has reached the end of its secularity. The majority of the population finds little of the moral and personal support once provided by the spirit of capitalism. The capitalist world is in disorder, spiritually as well as materially. What is there to believe in when the material world no longer furnishes us with spiritual rewards and sustenance?

In the process of its material development, capitalism has all but destroyed the sacred spirit. Our advanced secular society leaves us without the symbolism and belief to be a real part of this world. Without apprehending the infinite and eternal questions, we are not in this world. We have lost our hold; our qualities have become those of the barren landscape that surrounds us. That we do cope in this world says something about the persistence of the human spirit. That we can rise above the material and secular realm of capitalism attests to the prophetic possibilities in our own life and time.

But even our philosophy of being, as expressed most concisely in existential phenomenology, contains its own seeds of secularity. Being is always the possibility of being, a potential of being essentially in the world. The human, accordingly, "is always already in the future and turns the present into a means or a tool for the realization of projects."[25] Life is lived in anticipation, invalidating the present and fastening onto a future that is not yet. In the striving for essence, the human being is alienated from the actual; the present is to be overcome. In the existential life, human beings tend to negate their own activity, attempting to be "authentic."

Existential theology, likewise, builds on a separation between the realms of existence and essence. According to the existential theologian Rudolf Bultmann, the dichotomy upon which he bases his theology is as old as the beginning of Christianity:

> Whereas to ancient man the world has been home—in the Old Testament as God's creation, to classic Greece as the cosmos pervaded by the diety—the *utter difference of human existence from all worldly existence* was recognized for the first time in Gnosticism and Christianity, and thus the world became foreign soil to the human self.[26]

Bultmann then proceeds to construct a theology of existence based not on being but on the *potentiality to be*. True human being is conceived as possibility, as opposition to everything that is actual.[27] To be secure in one's existence, according to this existential theology, is to become worldly to the point of defining authentic being as radical potentiality. The emphasis is on a radical individuality, however, not on the creation of an authentic social existence.

The existential and secular trends are also represented in twentieth-century theologies. God is signified as "being-in-itself" in Tillich's neo-orthodox theology; Pierre Teilhard de

Chardin, the Jesuit theologian, emphasizes an evolutionary process of being in the universe; Bonhoeffer signals the "death of God" movement; and a secularized Christianity has developed divested of metaphysics, suggesting a world without God.[28]

In a continuation of twentieth-century trends, existential psychology has shattered the notion of a fixed human nature. In the social sciences, a belief in the relativity of cultures and social structures is the key to most analyses.[29] There is even the erosion, in the twentieth century, of the faith in science as the exemplar of all knowing. The contemporary trend represents the eclipse of God, self, and society—even of the possibility of knowing for certain about the world.

Yet, in spite of the trends in the social world and the trends in the imagination that lead to a void in the spirit, the need for a metaphysics of existence remains. The problem of metaphysics will not go away because of the basic human need to find a meaning that is not only of this world but that is transcendent as well. A symbolism is required that connects everyday existence to a meaning that infuses that existence with the fullness of being in the universe. No amount of meaning in the material world, however important and necessary, is sufficient or can replace the human capacity to ask questions about ultimate concerns. That we are beginning to ask such questions in our everyday lives and in our intellectual inquiry is a trend that is emerging dialectically in opposition to the twentieth-century trends of relativism and secularity.

Symbols in the Search for Meaning

We never outgrow the need for symbols in our lives. Even in the advance from capitalism to socialism, a symbolism that unites our social existence into a meaningful relationship with the universe is essential to the ontology of our being. The traditional religious symbolism of an earlier age no longer seems completely appropriate. At the same time, while traditional religious symbolism is being cast off, no symbolism has emerged with which to replace it. As a result we are being flung to the edges of the universe; we have nearly lost our way in the world. There is the concrete experience of our nonbeing, a sense of meaninglessness in the universe. We need a symbolism for our contemporary condition.

Our task as human beings—also our task as we exist in the world as intellectuals—is to create symbols for our age. We begin this task with the rethinking and recasting of the symbolism based on a traditional metaphysic. In the move toward a revised metaphysic, an alternative metaphysic based on existential and phenomenological categories has to be reconsidered as well. An existential phenomenology has appealed to the generations during the last half century because it provides a metaphysic for a world that is in flux and that has developed a sense of the relative and transitory nature of human existence. Such a philosophy allows us to negotiate the apparent ambiguities of the world. But more seems to be demanded of our philosophy and our belief in the emergence of a contemporary sensibility.

In broadest terms, we have reached a point in cultural-religious development that calls for a holistic metaphysic. There has been over the centuries a development from a monistic religious system to a radical dualism, followed by a questioning of that dualism and an affirmation of some version of metaphysical holism.[30] The ramifications pervade the material and nonmaterial elements of the entire culture. Focusing on these developments, Robert Bellah observes that at an earlier time (emerging in the first millennium B.C.) there was a "primitive religion" that exalted a reality apart from the actual world, a complete fusion of the mythical world with the world of everyday experience.[31] This was

followed by a period of "historic religion," in which a firm
dualism distinguished between a natural world and the supernatural. Dualism fostered a contrast between religious life
and political and social life. It reinforced the apparent contrast between a true realm of existence and everyday life.

The difference between "historic religion" and the more
recent development of "modern religion," Bellah continues,
is "the collapse of the dualism that was crucial to all the
historic religions."[32] Rather than a return to the monism of
primitive culture, modern religious culture is infused with a
multiplicity of symbols that attempt to unite the realms of
our existence. In modern culture there is an acceptance of
this world, but an acceptance that is demanded by the
imperative constantly to change the world in accordance with
the continuing emergence of consciousness.

This is not to argue that the traditional dualism of a
former culture has disappeared or that it cannot be part of a
modern symbolic system. Bellah writes: "I expect traditional
religious symbolism to be maintained and developed in new
directions, but with growing awareness that it is symbolism
and that man in the last analysis is responsible for the choice
of his symbolism."[33] To the extent that the traditional
symbolism is reappropriated, it likely will be recast into a
modern symbolism that emphasizes in some way the inter-
relation of all realms of existence. At any rate, it is not likely
that traditional symbolism will be simply reaffirmed, resort-
ing to the classic metaphysical dualism, but that we will
create a symbolic system that speaks to the wholeness of our
contemporary existence—and the transformation of our
social existence.

The ultimate—that which we have called and continue to
call the divine—is to be found in the everday life of social
existence and in our human history. All is related and essentially one. Specifically, everything in our culture is in some
way an expression of the religious situation.[34] As human and

socially creative production, culture is an expression of the ultimate—an enterprise of infinite importance. Religion is joined historically with all other realms of existence in the social and moral order of our society.

It is in the arena of everyday social and moral life—in our social existence—that the religious dimension of culture is realized. Thus, in our symbolic affairs there is no real distinction between the sacred and the secular. Yet there is the continuous attempt to divide the sacred and the secular into separate realms. While our ontological nature requires the presence of ultimate concern in all areas of life, the tendency is to establish a separate space for the religious, apart from the rest of the world. Nevertheless, the sacred and the secular are rooted in the experience of ultimate concern, that of searching for meaning in our lives in relation to the totality of meaning in the universe.

Our search is directed to a symbolism—to a life—that finds the core of meaning in the human community, in our social existence. Beyond the existential image of human action, beyond the idolatry of the human individual, we seek a grounding in the ontology of our social existence. Beyond any dualism of this world and another, we find our meaning in the everyday experience of transforming the world according to the creative and divine possibilities of our social being. The ancient split between secular wisdom and a sacred faith is thereby overcome in the struggle for social existence. Regained is the dimension of depth in our encounter with reality. Together we are creating a world.

NOTES

1. Lao Tzu, *Tao Te Ching*, as quoted in Peter Matthiessen, *The Snow Leopard* (New York: Viking, 1978), p. 65.

40   SOCIAL EXISTENCE

2. Genesis 1:1-3, *The Holy Bible*, Revised Standard Version.

3. For the historical transformation of *logos*, as especially revealed in the Johannine gospel, see Rudolf Bultmann, *The Gospel of John: A Commentary*, trans. G. R. Beasley-Murray (Oxford: Blackwell, 1971), pp. 13-83.

4. Saint Augustine, *On Christian Doctrine*, trans. D. W. Robertson, Jr. (Indianapolis: Bobbs-Merrill, 1958), p. 14.

5. *Ibid.*, p. 133.

6. Dietrich Bonhoeffer, *Ethics*, ed. Eberhard Bethge (New York: Macmillan, 1955), p. 19.

7. Walter Benjamin, *Reflections: Essays, Aphorisms, Autobiographical Writings*, trans. Edmund Jephcott (New York: Harcourt Brace Jovanovich, 1978), p. 323.

8. Martin Heidegger, "Being and Time," *Basic Writings*, ed. David Farrell Krell (New York: Harper & Row, 1977), pp. 45-50.

9. Martin Heidegger, "Letter on Humanism," *ibid.*, pp. 228-229.

10. Hans-Georg Gadamer, *Philosophical Hermeneutics*, trans. and ed. David E. Linge (Berkeley: University of California Press, 1976), esp. pp. 198-240.

11. Søren Kierkegaard, *The Concept of Dread*, trans. Walter Lowrie (Princeton: Princeton University Press, 1957).

12. Rollo May, *The Meaning of Anxiety*, 2nd ed. (New York: Pocket Books, 1977), p. xxi. On Heidegger's earlier and related discussion, see John Macquarrie, *Existenialism* (New York: Penguin, 1972), pp. 164-171.

13. Paul Tillich, *The Courage to Be* (New Haven: Yale University Press, 1952), p. 35.

14. *Ibid.*, p. 47.

15. See the discussion of the existential concept of care in John Macquarrie, *An Existential Theology: A Comparison of Heidegger and Bultmann* (New York: Macmillan, 1955), pp. 112-116.

16. Paul Tillich, *The Socialist Decision*, trans. Franklin Sherman (New York: Harper & Row, 1977), p. 108.

17. Paul Tillich, *Theology of Culture*, ed. Robert C. Kimball (New York: Oxford University Press, 1959), pp. 118-119.

18. Especially Karl Marx, *Grundrisse: Foundations of the Critique of Political Economy*, trans. Martin Nicolaus (New York: Random House, 1973).

19. Paul Tillich, *The Protestant Era* (Chicago: University of Chicago Press, 1948), p. 60.

20. See Shlomo Avineri, *The Social and Political Thought of Karl Marx* (London: Cambridge University Press, 1969), pp. 202-249.

21. Tillich, *The Socialist Decision*, p. 109.

22. Karel Kosík, *Dialectics of the Concrete: A Study on Problems of Man and World* (Boston: D. Reidel, 1976), p. 7.

23. Dietrich Bonhoeffer, *Letters and Papers from Prison*, ed. Eberhard Bethge (New York: Macmillan, 1966), pp. 194-195.

24. Franklin L. Baumer, *Modern European Thought: Continuity and Change in Ideas, 1600-1950* (New York: Macmillan, 1977), p. 439.

25. Kosík, *Dialectics of the Concrete*, p. 42.

26. Rudolf Bultmann, *Theology of the New Testament*, Vol. 1, trans. Kendrick Grobel (New York: Scribner, 1951), p. 165.

27. See Robert C. Roberts, *Rudolf Bultmann's Theology: A Critical Interpretation* (Grand Rapids: Eerdmans, 1976), esp. pp. 21-59.

28. See Baumer, *Modern European Thought*, pp. 439-455; Alasdair MacIntyre, *Secularization and Moral Change* (London: Oxford University Press, 1967), pp. 66-76.

29. The modern version of existentialism in sociology is contained in Jack D. Douglas and John M. Johnson (eds.), *Existential Sociology* (New York: Cambridge University Press, 1977).

30. Richard Quinney, *Providence: The Reconstruction of Social and Moral Order* (New York: Longman, 1980). See George Rupp, *Beyond Existentialism and Zen: Religion in a Pluralistic World* (New York: Oxford University Press, 1979), pp. 27-46.

31. Robert Bellah, *Beyond Belief: Essays in Religion in a Post-Traditional World* (New York: Harper & Row, 1970), pp. 20-50.

32. *Ibid.*, p. 40.

33. *Ibid.*, p. 42.

34. Tillich, *Theology of Culture*, pp. 40-51.

2

The Problem
of Reality

Our creation of a world is at once an understanding of the reality we confront and grasp in our lives and the transformation of that reality. In the understanding and the acting we find a meaning in reality. The human project is to understand reality in the course of creating it, to create reality in the course of understanding it.

What is, is there, whether or not we take as our project to understand and transform it. But reality becomes a world—a "social reality," a reality of human significance—when it is understood and acted upon. For human purposes, then, reality is that which is appropriated and comprehended in the context of our lives.

Social reality is more than that which we consciously attend to in our everyday lives. Once created, it gives structure to life, whether or not we consciously grasp the existence and meaning of that structure. There is a structure of reality (including elements that are social, economic, and political) that is there for our understanding, a structure that is constantly changing as we understand and act upon it. Social reality is thus within the structure of our historical condition. As Karl Marx noted, social beings make their own history, "but they do not make it just as they please; they do not make it under circumstances chosen by themselves, but under circumstances directly encountered, given and transmitted from the past."[1] The structural reality, as historically constructed, provides the setting for realizing the possibilities of transformation.

Already, in a brief introduction to the persistent problem of reality, we have alluded to several levels of reality. There is (1) the *natural-supernatural reality* of the physical universe, (2) the *everyday social reality* of human social activity, and (3) the *structured social reality* that is constructed historically and is known to us in varying degrees. The complexity of reality easily gives rise to the tendency to divide the world into distinct realms of existence. Part of our developing consciousness, however, involves an understanding of the complexity of reality. When all of the realms of reality are conceived holistically in social terms, in word and in action, we speak of *social existence*. Meaning is then to be found in social existence.

Beyond Appearance versus Reality

As much as we may divide reality into separate realms, reality is a *totality*. Any type of phenomenon that we may want to select for investigation can be conceived as a moment of the whole. Because reality is a whole, any phenomenon is our understanding of its place (including its contradictory place) in the whole. Such is the *dialectical* conception of the totality of reality: depicting "reality as a whole that is not only a sum of relations, facts and processes, but is also the very process of forming them, their structure and their genesis."[2] Reality is always in the process of formation, becoming known to us as human social beings in the course of our praxis of living in the world.

But our intellectual and religious tradition tends to suggest otherwise. We have held a dualistic view of reality, separating the historical from the transhistorical, this world from the other world, nature from human life, and the appearances of this world from a true reality. This has been essentially the Judeo-Christian world view, the Pauline view that is written in the epistle: "For this slight momentary affliction is preparing for us an eternal weight of glory beyond all comparison, because we look not to the things that are seen but to the things that are unseen; for the things that are seen are transient, but the things that are unseen are eternal" (2 Corinthians 4:17-18).

In the Johannine gospel, as well, there is a dualism that continues to pervade our world view. The message is that we are *in* the world but not *of* the world. It is held, in existential terms, that our existence is bound up with the world but that we are not part of it as physical objects are part of it.[3] On the other hand, to become merged in the world—without being able to detach ourselves from all the material aspects of life—is to have an inauthentic existence, losing ourselves in the world. With such thinking the dualism of the Judeo-Christian tradition has been integrated into Western existentialism.

The New Testament view, however, does not necessarily end with all salvation taking place in another world, in an eternity. The gospel according to John contains two levels of drama. There is, of course, the heavenly world apart from the earthly world. But there is also a world of redeeming possibilities that is neither mystical nor otherworldly. As the biblical theologian J. Louis Martyn observed in a reading of the text, "John has Jesus modify the traditional hope for rooms in heaven by speaking about a home on earth."[4] The drama of an otherworldly eschatology infuses meaning into the events of this world. "And the word became flesh and dwelt among us, full of grace and truth; we have beheld his glory, glory as of the only Son from the Father" (John 1:14). Martyn thus concludes:

The two-level drama makes clear that the Word's dwelling among us and our beholding his glory are not events which transpired only in the past. They do not constitute an ideal period when the kingdom of God was on earth, a period to which one looks back with the knowledge that it has now drawn to a close with Jesus' ascension to heaven as the Son of Man. These events to which John bears witness transpire on both the *einmalig* and the contemporary levels of the drama, or they do not transpire at all. In John's view, their transpiring on both levels of the drama is, to a large extent, the good news itself.[5]

The dualism of the Judeo-Christian tradition—and as incorporated into Western intellectual thought—contains a powerful dialectic that gives essential (and ultimate) meaning to human social existence.

Dualism in its various forms, however, is increasingly being critically reevaluated. The task is difficult, as is the change required in the way life is lived, because dualism is so basic to our conventional wisdom. I have found the duality of existence and essence to be important in understanding the world and in the struggle to transform it. Especially useful and meaningful has been the interplay between the essential possibilities of this world and a notion of the essence of an infinite existence, between the earthly kingdom and the heavenly kingdom. Some kind of modification or revision is necessary in the traditional dualism. If we retain some aspects of this dualism, we must at least do so without the innocence of the past. A dualism in the world can no longer be taken for granted.

The arguments advanced by Hannah Arendt in her book *Thinking* have been particularly important to me in questioning the traditional dualism we hold regarding the perception of reality. She suggests that the distinction between being ("true being") and appearance ("mere appearance"), as conventionally posed, has come to an end—is "dead":

What has come to an end is the basic distinction between the sensory and the suprasensory, together with the notion, at least as old as Parmenides, that whatever is not given to the senses—God or Being or the First Principles and Causes (*archai*) or the Ideas—is more real, more truthful, more meaningful than what appears, that it is not just *beyond* sense perception but *above* the world of the senses. What is "dead" is not only the localization of such "eternal truths" but also the distinction itself.[6]

Once the suprasensory realm is discarded, the world of appearances as understood for centuries is annihilated.

The *two-world theory* provided the framework for thinking about and acting upon reality. With the breakdown of the theory, Arendt notes, nothing seems to make much sense any more. Especially precarious is the status of that which is invisible and soundless, including thinking and believing. Is there a home in the world for anything that does not appear concretely, that lies beyond our sense of sight and sound? Arendt's contention that "the two-world theory belongs among the metaphysical fallacies" obviously takes us to new and troublesome places.[7] Questions about the meaning of social existence take on new meaning.

Appearance, in spite of its questionable fate in the two-world theory, is a fact of everyday life. There is the relentless search for that ("the cause") which lies beneath the appearance—a search in our everyday life as well as in the scientific enterprise. There is the conviction that appearances must have grounds that are more than appearances. But Arendt argues, "The belief that a cause should be of higher rank than the effect (so that an effect can easily be disparaged by being retraced to its cause) may belong to the oldest and most stubborn metaphysical fallacies."[8] There is occurring in modern science, however, a revision in the relation of cause and effect, true reality and appearance.

Emerging is the argument that "appearances are no longer depreciated as 'secondary qualities' but understood as necessary conditions for essential processes that go on inside the living organism."[9] Appearances may not, accordingly, exist for the life process, but the life process may exist for the sake of the appearances. "Since we live in an *appearing* world, is it not much more plausible that the relevant and the meaningful in this world of ours should be located precisely on the surface?"[10] The surface, in other worlds, is becoming as essential in our thinking and acting as that which lives beneath it; what we "are" is as important as what is "inside"; the outside is more than an illusion. Arendt quotes W. H. Auden: "Does God ever judge us by appearances? I suspect he does."

Although our current language is inadequate to the task of incorporating a revised notion of appearance and reality into a comprehensive system, we can begin to imagine the possibilities. Arendt suggests that it is plausible to conclude that "there may indeed exist a fundamental ground behind an appearing world, but that this ground's chief and even sole significance lies in its effects, that is, in what it causes to appear, rather than in its sheer creativity."[11] We may still hold to the philosophical understanding of being as the ground of appearance, but this is not to maintain the antagonism in the evaluation of being *versus* appearance that is inherent in the two-world theory.

Our ordinary experience suggests the importance of appearances. It is the thinking ego that tends to make the antagonistic separation between true being and appearance. The problem then becomes one of developing a critical form of thought that is capable of distinguishing the relative importance of the particular appearance.[12] A critical form of thought emerges in the living of a critical life. Reality is the union of ontological being and social existence. Only in an isolation produced by the imagination could the one become separated into two, and only then could either type of reality be regarded as more important than the other.

If the separation is made in our thought, it is for the purpose of a particular kind of understanding and action. It is legitimate (and necessary), for instance, to consider the distinction between existence and essence when a critical judgment is to be made on the authenticity (or the possibilities) of a particular existence. Then the essence of things—the "thing itself" that is not directly and immediately observable—can be understood and used critically to evaluate everyday, concrete existence. The ultimate meaning of phenomena becomes known as the product of everyday praxis—thus joining existence and essence, appearance and true reality.[13] The meaning of the essential qualities of existence are found only in existence itself. In our critical thinking we may know the separation; and critical thinking makes available, once again, the union. In a critical life we recreate the whole. Reality is thereby transformed.

In other words, the world is understood—given meaning—in the forms of living and thinking that move back and forth between rationally parceling the world into levels of reality and intuitively joining them again holistically. The separating and the uniting are two different forms of thought and praxis for achieving understanding and for producing a transformation in existence. Critical theory in its rationalistic and intuitive forms is a way of finding and giving meaning to social existence. It is a way, to use the metaphor, of knowing the word.

The sensibility of the modern (or "postmodern") world places particular emphasis on overcoming the dualism of separate realities. The unknown spiritual order is to be united with our concrete and immediate experiences. The earth and the heavens are no longer divided, but the earth is in the heavens and heaven is on earth. Ultimately there is no division, and all the theological and everyday notions based on the distinction collapse with the realization. There is a union in the universe and a union in our experience. We no longer look for a spiritual order outside of our experience; the spiritual is within our experience and the experience is within the spiritual. The unknown in the universe is within us and we are part of the unknown of the universe.

On Form and Beauty

That we begin with appearance and then move to an understanding of what appears is the traditional imagery of the knowing process. The world of appearance, the phenomenal world, is prior to whatever understanding we want to develop. This is our tradition:

> In order to find out what truly *is*, the philosopher must *leave* the world of appearances among which he is naturally and originally at home—as Parmenides did when he was carried upward, beyond the gates of night and day, to the divine way that lay "far from the beaten path of men," and as Plato did, too, in the Cave parable.[14]

The philosopher takes leave of the world of existence to find the deeper meaning of life—moving out of the cave of human affairs in order truly to know.

By moving away from human experience to the realm of pure and rational thought, Plato argued, the philosopher could come to know the essence of things. Reason allows the knower to move outside the senses (the body) to a knowledge that emanates from a divine element in the soul. Whereas sensory experience is superficial and deceptive, human reason (the eye of the mind) is able to know infallibly the essential *forms* that are separated from the phenomenal. Knowledge is to be clearly distinguished from sensory awareness. There is, furthermore, a *beauty* that is universal and eternal, in a knowledge based on innate form.

For Plato, and generally for the rationalist tradition that followed, knowing is a bringing together of the form and the world of experience. Plato wrote in *Phaedrus:* "It is impossible for a soul that has never seen the truth to enter into our human shape; it takes a man to understand by the use of universals, and to collect out of the multiplicity of sense-impressions a unity arrived at by a process of reason."[15] The process of reason, he continues in the same passage, "is simply the recollection of things which our soul once perceived when it took its journey with a god, looking down from above on the things to which we now ascribe reality and gazing upwards towards what is truly real."

Furthermore, for Plato, the process of knowing is an aesthetic one: that which is known through reason (in the recollection of innate form) is a manifestation of beauty. When we know beauty in the world, according to Plato's rationalism, we know what is real and universal. To find beauty in the world is to partake of divinity, to be reminded by the sight of beauty on earth of true beauty. The beauty that we know is an imitation of the beauty in the eternal and universal forms. Finally, as Plato points out in *The Symposium,* love is the link between the sensible and the eternal, the conscious need for the beautiful and the good. All human beings, in other words, given the innate need, are lovers. "One desires what one lacks."[16] Love, for Plato, is the search for wisdom and beauty, and beauty in wisdom.

Rationalist thought provides the basis not only for the secular pursuit of knowledge but for much of religion as well. The Good—that which is in the universal form—is also divine. Several centuries after Plato, Augustine, in the transition between classical civilization and the Middle Ages, helped forge an intellectual and spiritual tradition that remained in

effect for the next thousand years. That tradition continued
the search for eternal forms, now very much in religious
terms. In a concise statement of the presence of the universal
whole, beyond the fact of making a human world, Augustine
wrote:

> The world and the work of divine creation whereby
> human nature comes to be what it is in each person is
> eternal and thus ever-present. Through the memory of
> what is essentially present, the mind has access to that
> relationship and love wherein the mind is fashioned
> after the image of God. So long as the mind is forgetful
> of this relationship and dwells apart from this love, the
> mind is deformed, which deformity is experienced as
> personal misery and restlessness. In his misery, one's
> question is one's quest for blessedness.[17]

The universal form was now conceived as the image of God, a
Christian God. The religious as well as intellectual search is
divine—and a source of salvation.

The search is firmly established in Christian theology. The
great theologian and religious leader of the Great Awakening
in New England in the middle of the eighteenth century,
Jonathan Edwards, made the aesthetic of truth and beauty a
central part of his theology. Beauty, in fact, is the first
principle of being in Edwards's system, "the inner, structural
principle of being itself, according to which the universal
system of being is articulated."[18] Beauty is the measure and
foundation of goodness—the basis for affirming the ultimate
unity of being and good in God. Beauty is God's perfection;
and it is spiritual beauty that constitutes the image of God in
human beings. A student of Edwards's theology observes,
finally, that "virtue, both natural and spiritual, and all varieties of justice and fruits of conscience are understood by
him as varieties and forms of beauty."[19] God governs, accord-

ing to Edwards, not by brute force but by the beauty of the good. Beauty is the order of the universe.

The flight taken with the gods to the source of all truth and beauty is evident in human pursuits with secular as well as with religious purpose. Poetry, for instance, becomes the means of escape to another world in the imaginative and artistic search for beauty and truth. John Keats took flight in his poetics:

> I am certain of nothing but of the holiness of the Heart's affections and the truth of Imagination. What the Imagination seizes as Beauty must be truth—whether it existed before or not—for I have the same idea of all our passions as of Love: they are all, in the sublime, creative of essential Beauty.[20]

A sense of beauty in the heart, in Keats and other romantic poets and artists, is thus capable of transporting the artist beyond the world of action and social reality. The Romantic movement in the arts, although alternately detaching itself from the world, contained a critique of the world (industrializing capitalism) in its ability to see beyond it to a higher form of beauty and truth.[21] Through the artistic impulse another possibility for human existence could be imagined.

Rationalist philosophy continues to provide us with a heightened sense of the search for wisdom, beauty, and justice. We are filled with the Greek *eros*, the desire for what is not but what could be. We contemplate and struggle for the supreme form, the good. Whether transcendence is purely in terms of human and social betterment on earth or is an attempt to find God's will in sacred terms, the quest is for the ultimate and absolute good.[22] A recognition of (or belief in) a universal form or ontological being is the foundation of our thought and action even at the end of the twentieth century.

We return to the problem of the two-world theory in a consideration of form and beauty: true reality versus appearance. Rationalist thought leads us to place primary value on the world beyond us. But this need not be the case. We may still hold to the distinction between the appearance of everyday life and the ultimate forms that lie beyond without giving primacy to either. In the aesthetic of the beautiful as a reflection of ultimate form we lay hold to the good. In the beauty of the appearance truth becomes visible. As the phenomenologist Hans-Georg Gadamer observes:

> Obviously it is the distinguishing mark of the beautiful over against the good that of itself it presents itself, that it makes itself immediately apparent in its being. This means that it has the most important ontological function: that of mediating between idea and appearance.[23]

The beautiful is visibly present to the senses, and in the connection with universal forms sense experience and rationality are joined into a whole. In aesthetics the unity of appearance and ontological reality is made manifest. We find truth—the meaning of our existence—the moment beauty in the world becomes evident. And it is only in this world of everyday life that we come to know beauty.

In our lives we experience the union of appearance (beauty) and true reality (form). We know when there is a harmony between an activity and the truth or goodness of that activity. Such insights emerge, as the psychoanalyst Rollo May suggests, "because they have a certain form, the form that is beautiful because it completes an incomplete Gestalt."[24] The answer comes to us not through pure reason, nor through pure sense perception, passion, or intuition, but through the conscious union of the form that now presents itself, organizing momentarily an otherwise incomplete experience of the world—a found beauty in itself:

The choice is not necessarily between the epistemology of the rational thought of rationalism or the sensory perception of empiricism. If a choice is made it is only for particular and immediate purposes. But there is a union (or a blending) of the epistemologies into a whole.[25] Human knowledge and human life are a mixture of experience and reason, into a whole, with no determinable primacy given to either experience or reason. Neither faculty—if we could separate them—precedes the other or is of greater importance. In our everyday lives we constantly develop a language and a consciousness that provide the context for speaking about truth and struggling for the good. At any moment we take on faith—through the appearance of the beautiful—the correctness and rightness of our thoughts and actions. Thus, there is the necessary relation of believing and knowing in the whole of our being.

Believing and Knowing

We continue to ask: How do we, as commonsense beings, come to know the reality of our existence? Even with the union of sense experience and the rationality of form—in beauty—there remains the problem of understanding reality. Our senses and our reasoning abilities may combine into the whole that allows us to apprehend the world, but to understand the *meaning* of that grasping requires another faculty of the mind and spirit. Let us now, then, pursue an epistemology that adds to our sense experience and to our rationality the faculty of *belief.* We may experience and we may know, but we do not truly understand the meaning of reality until we also believe. To know we must believe, and in believing and knowing we come to understand the meaning of our existence.

I assume that we think and that we question the meaning
of our existence for reasons that go beyond the pure desire to
know for its own sake. We are caught, instead, in a passion
that surpasses intellectualizing. Our knowing is caught up by
the ultimate question of our being. Tillich writes, "Reason is
overpowered, invaded, shaken by the ultimate concern."[26]
When we ask questions about the meaning of our existence
("Why is there something? Why not nothing?") we are
pushed to the very roots of our existence. Our reflection is in
the ultimate sense. Understanding is for the purpose of coming to terms with our life and our finitude, seeking the
dimension of the eternal that is in our human being and in
the human social forms we create in order to realize the
eternal quality of our being.

Much of modern thinking—at least that narrow range of
thought embodied in the social sciences—does not attend to
the profound questions of being and existence. Certainly a
language and a symbolism that incorporates the divine character of existence is excluded from modern secular thought.
In this sense, modern thought is atheistic, whether excluded
is a godhead symbolism or a symbolism that speaks to other
conceptions of the divine. The divine word is certainly all but
absent from modern social theory. Yet, there remains at the
core of modern thinking—as embodied in theological reflection, much of philosophy, and much of everyday thinking—a
faithfulness to the divine word. "What is definitively modern," notes Robert Meagher in his study of Augustine, "is the
claim and the experience of the identity of the human word
and the divine word."[27] In our contemporary sensibility is
the search for a language and a symbolism that will allow us
to understand the reality of our existence.

The search for meaning in relation to a symbolism of the
word is not simply the application of belief to observation.
The search is *dialectical*, requiring a scrutiny of everything we
believe in and live by. The dialectical metaphor (whether

describing the philosopher, minister, teacher, or deity) is of "the good physician," who tells the "patients what they *don't* want to hear in the hope that by forcing them to see themselves clearly, they may be moved to change the selves they see."[28] The self and all knowing are consumed in response to the purging qualities of the dialectic. The value of the inquiry, the literary theorist Stanley E. Fish observes, "is determined less by its truth-content than by its effectiveness in stimulating further inquiry and thereby contributing to the progressive illumination of the aspiring mind."[29] What takes place, as Augustine argued, is a total reorientation or conversion of being. Whatever text we are reading—Scripture, secular scripts, or the world of everyday life—the dialectic is in effect in our understanding.

The dialectical way of reading the text—and of understanding the world—is also a way of living that is attuned to questions of ultimate meaning. In his discussion of the dialectic in Augustine, Fish writes:

Translated into a rule for living, this means that as we proceed through our allotted three-score-and-ten, everything we encounter is to be interpreted (and valued) not with reference to the appearance it makes in any earthly configuration, but with reference to its function in the larger design of God's providential dispensation; and every commitment into which we enter is to be regarded either as temporary or as a shadow of our greater and overriding commitment to Him. In short, we are to live in time, but for (the sake of) eternity, seeking always to discern and respond to God's meaning rather than to the meaning that leaps immediately to our carnal eyes.[30]

History and our current experiences are signs of the divine in our everyday lives. The ultimate significance of existence is found in our social existence, living in the search for the meaning of that existence.

The dialectic of our believing and knowing demands a reconstruction in thought and practice. Whereas method bypasses the soul, performing certain mechanical operations, the dialectic requires a reorientation. The dialectic

> is soul-centered; the response it requires is decisional (in the religious or existential sense) and its effects are long-lasting because the changes they work are basic. Dialectic asks not for reform or restraint, but for revolution; it does not polish, but purges; it does not delay, but extirpates self-satisfaction; it does not make the mind capable, but unmakes the mind. Method reduces all minds to a common level, the level of empirical observation. Dialectic raises the level of the mind, and raises it to the point where it becomes indistinguishable from the object of its search, and so disappears.[31]

We are approaching the epistemological territory of the Augustinian recognition: that in order to know we must believe. Even that which we call science or scientific knowledge is open to the invisible and less tangible structures of the universe. Indeed, a recent philosopher of science writes: "It is with an ability to apprehend greater imperceptible and intangible magnitudes that recent science has penetrated more deeply. There is a fundamental kinship between the wonder and awe of worship and the dialogue of science with the realities of the universe."[32] A new paradigm is emerging, consisting of a revised epistemology, one that brings believing and knowing together for the task of understanding the meaning of the universe and all that is within it. The dualism of belief and knowledge will not persist as belief and knowledge are joined into a single paradigm of understanding. The result will be a culture that is capable of inspiring and directing its destiny in accordance with the eternal. Human history becomes a drama and a struggle of ultimate purpose.

In the unity of believing and knowing there is the understanding of the larger purpose of our lives in the universe—that life is directed toward the providential construction of the world. The source and goal of all matter and life are in the unfolding of the universe, that which we variously call providence, God, Being-beyond-all-being, the power or order in the universe. This is an epistemology that is recognizably theological. Believing and knowing are guided by an understanding that has as its aim a concern for the implicit unity of existence. This is, in particular, the understanding proposed by Jonathan Edwards, drawing from our own prophetic tradition: "He that sees the beauty of holiness, or true moral good, sees the greatest and most important thing in the world, which is the fulness of all things, without which all the world is empty, yea, worse than nothing." [33] All understanding is in the larger perspective of the providential nature of the universe. The presence of purpose is found in the reality of everyday life and in the structures we create (consciously and otherwise) to fulfill our existence.

What is known, therefore, depends on what is believed to be the purpose of existence. All understanding takes place in the nexus of believing and knowing. There can be no understanding without the aim of knowing for a purpose. Because we care, we desire to know. We do not begin to know *tabula rasa*; we are active knowers, not passive: "Mostly we know when we enjoy, love, praise, and care for the things around us." [34] The understanding that results from such believing and knowing is the appropriate understanding of reality.

Understanding—as integral to being human—thus takes as its aim the pursuit of the good. Understanding and the action that relates to that understanding exemplify our particular nature as human social beings. Understanding and social action are ultimately directed, returning to the classical

Greek notion: "The good towards which we recognize the idea of life as aiming is the good towards which we ought to understand every art, action, and pursuit as aiming, including the art of inquiring, into this good."[35] Such understanding, based on knowing and believing, is a way of existing. It is fundamental to our personal and social existence.

Hermeneutics and the
Meaning of Reality

We must believe in order to understand. Yet, it is only by understanding that we can believe. This is the problem of hermeneutics—of interpretation and understanding—that Paul Ricoeur refers to as the "knot," appearing as the hermeneutical circle.[36] The circle, rather than being vicious, is a vital and stimulating one. It is in the circle that we begin to regain that which has been lost, with the facility of interpretive criticism of which we are capable. The symbols around us give meaning and criticism interprets.

We have to believe before we can understand: "Never, in fact, does the interpreter get near to what his text says unless he lives in the *aura* of the meaning he is inquiring after."[37] All understanding (that is, interpretation) is guided by the manner in which the question is posed and the aim of the inquiry. All understanding, consequently, is directed by a prior understanding of the problem to which we are attending. And, in the other portion of the circle, we must understand in order to believe; interpretation helps us to find meaning again. Such is the creative circle of believing and understanding in hermeneutics: "hermeneutics proceeds from a prior understanding of the very thing that it tries to understand by interpreting it."[38]

We can no longer, however, believe in the symbolism of the sacred that once provided the foundation of the meaning of reality. What we moderns or postmoderns are left with is interpretive understanding. The hermeneutic allows us to *hear* again. Ricoeur poetically captures the modern desire and possibility: "It is not regret for the sunken Atlantides that animates us, but hope for a recreation of language. Beyond the desert of criticism, we wish to be called again."[39]

The meaning of reality comes to us only through prior faith in that reality. Without a belief—that is, without symbols that give meaning to the world—it is impossible to construct a new and appropriate meaning of our existence. With faith, in contrast, there are symbols that furnish the basis for creating a new interpretation, an understanding of our existence as experienced in contemporary times. We are now at the beginning of a reconstruction; the world is being revealed to us. There is a revelation, an apprehension of an order in the universe.[40] In the revelation, a faith is offered to us, the necessary basis for interpretation and for the creation of a meaningful reality in our age.

The symbolic world within which we interpret and understand the meaning of our social existence is given to us through the medium of language. Hence, Gadamer writes, "language is the real medium of human being, if we only see it in the realm that it alone fills out, the realm of human being-together, the realm of common understanding, or ever-replenished common agreement—a realm as indispensable to human life as the air we breathe."[41] Human beings—in a covenant with each other and with the *logos* of the universe—think, speak, and communicate their very being through their own words. A world of shared meanings with ultimate concerns is created by means of language. The words and symbols of our particular language reveal to us our special being at this point in the history of being human: "The language of a time is not so much chosen by the persons who use it as it is their historical fate—the way being has revealed itself to and concealed itself from them as their starting point."[42]

The task of interpretive understanding—whether in everyday language usage or in explicit hermeneutical reflection—is
"to hearken to and bring to language the possibilities that are
suggested but remain unspoken in what the tradition speaks
to us."[43] In all of our human activities we are attempting to
render unto the world an understanding. Every historical
situation elicits new attempts to understand the world
through language, to render the world into language, drawing
from our tradition and trying at the same time to go beyond
it.

It is through human language that the invisibles become
manifest. As human beings, Arendt notes, we "have an *urge
to speak* and thus to make manifest what otherwise would
not be part of the appearing world at all."[44] And the urge to
speak is prompted by the human need for meaning. We think
by means of language, and we construct meaning in our lives
in the course of our communication through language. We are
in a meaningful social existence because of the word. Human
language is the link between the word in the universe and our
understanding in our own words. Meaning is revealed to us
within our own particular historical situation.

Language, then, is the universal medium in which understanding is made possible and is realized. In the language
given in the historical tradition, communicated daily with
others, interpretation of the world takes place. Interpretation
is essentially the understanding that is demanded in being
human. The problems of language and interpretation, as
Gadamer observes, are the problems of understanding: "All
understanding is interpretation, and all interpretation takes
place in the medium of language, which would allow the
object to come into words and yet is at the same time the
interpreter's own language."[45] The meaning of existence, in
other words, if found only in our social existence and our
conscious understanding of that existence. In daily life we
find the meaning that is at once finite and eternal.

Language, then, has everything to do with social existence. There is no language apart from the historical situation within which language develops and the social context within which it is communicated. Language, with all the speaking and interpretation, is a communal endeavor; social existence, and an understanding of that existence, is accomplished through the medium of language. With all of its explicit and hidden signs and symbols, language is a medium of practical activity. There is no meaning to the exclusion of the practical involvements of human beings in social life.[46] Likewise, there is no understanding of the meaning of social existence without an immersion in the language of the particular society in which we live. Whether the hermeneutical task is a "professional" one (primarily as observer) or one of everyday life (as participant), we are firmly within the symbolic realm of our everyday language. The hermeneutic of interpretation and understanding is a commonsense activity.

Hermeneutical reflection (in everyday life and in the philosophical enterprise) achieves its essential purpose when it reflects simultaneously on its own critical endeavors. In critical reflection, not only is the process of understanding put into question, but also questioned is the social world of lived existence. Beginning within the commonsense tradition, yet critically reflecting upon it, interpretation moves to the hidden possibilities of the tradition (yet to be realized) and to the construction of possibilities beyond that tradition—changing the tradition itself. Critical understanding is critical existence. The critical meaning of social existence is found in the struggle for social existence.

The understanding that is known through the word is both a disclosure and a creation. Coming out of both the Greek and the Judeo-Christian tradition, the hermeneutic of our everyday life seeks simultaneously to hear the word of the universal order and to speak and act in a way that will make the world anew.[47] There is the re-creation of the divine out of an understanding of the divine that is given. The human word and the divine word become one; the creative word spoken at the beginning of time is disclosed and becomes the source of constructing social existence in our time. "All proper human speech is prophecy in which the eternal word sounds forth," we are reminded, through the always temporal (and always social) human word.[48]

In another age the human word was a manifestation of God's will, of God acting in the universe and in human history. The human word and the word of God were inseparable; human words were charged with the divine. A recent observer of Jonathan Edwards's theology of language can write about the linguistic sensibility of that time:

> Language is not simply a set of figures of speech or apt metaphors in a speaker's rhetorical flight; it is a mind's renewing apprehension of its world and a fresh insight into reality. Language is, therefore, the handiwork of God in His history and another dimension of His world.[49]

For the modern sensibility, however, another language of the ultimate source and creative possibility of the word is necessary. Once again we are in the vital search for the meaning of reality; there is the awful problem of reality. The search—and the struggle that is integral to it—involves a way of speaking and way of understanding our human social existence.

NOTES

1. Karl Marx, *The Eighteenth Brumaire of Louis Bonaparte* (New York: International, 1963), p. 15.

2. Karel Kosík, *Dialectics of the Concrete: A Study on Problems of Man and World* (Boston: D. Reidel, 1976), pp. 23-24.

3. See John Macquarrie, *An Existential Theology: A Comparison of Heidegger and Bultmann* (New York: Macmillan, 1955), pp. 39-47.

4. J. Louis Martyn, *History and Theology in the Fourth Gospel*, 2nd ed. (Nashville: Abingdon, 1979), p. 148.

5. *Ibid.*, pp. 150-151.

6. Hannah Arendt, *Thinking* (New York: Harcourt Brace Jovanovich, 1978), p. 10.

7. *Ibid.*, p. 22.

8. *Ibid.*, p. 25.

9. *Ibid.*, p. 27.

10. *Ibid.*

11. *Ibid.*, p. 42.

12. *Ibid.*, p. 45.

13. On praxis in relation to thinking about appearance and reality, see Kosík, *Dialectics of the Concrete*, pp. 1-17.

14. Arendt, *Thinking*, p. 23.

15. Plato, *Phaedrus and the Seventh and Eighth Letters*, trans. Walter Hamilton (New York: Penguin, 1973), p. 55.

16. Plato, *The Symposium*, trans. Walter Hamilton (New York: Penguin, 1951), p. 76.

17. Augustine, as quoted in Rogert E. Meagher, *Augustine: An Introduction* (New York: New York University Press, 1978), p. 141.

18. Ronald André Delattre, *Beauty and Sensibility in the Thought of Jonathan Edwards: An Essay in Aesthetics and Theological Ethics* (New Haven: Yale University Press, 1968), pp. 1-2.

19. *Ibid.*, p. 2.

20. John Keats, as quoted in E. P. Thompson, *William Morris: Romantic to Revolutionary* (New York: Pantheon, 1976), p. 19.

21. As argued and documented by E. P. Thompson, *ibid.*, passim.

22. On the place of *eros* in Christianity, see Louis Dupré, *The Other Dimension: A Search for the Meaning of Religious Attitudes* (Garden City: Doubleday, 1972), pp. 112-147.

23. Hans-Georg Gadamer, *Truth and Method* (New York: Seabury Press, 1975), p. 438.

24. Rollo May, *The Courage to Create* (New York: Bantam, 1976), p. 74.

25. See the essay by Richard I. Aaron, "Epistemology," *Encyclopedia Britannica*, Vol. 6 (Chicago: Encyclopedia Britannica, 1975), pp. 925-948.

26. Paul Tillich, *Systematic Theology*, Vol. 1 (Chicago: University of Chicago Press, 1951), p. 53. See the discussion by Rollo May, *Paulus: Reminiscence of a Friendship* (New York: Harper & Row, 1973), pp. 12-24.

27. Meagher, *Augustine*, p. 27.

28. Stanley E. Fish, *Self-Consuming Artifacts: The Experience of Seventeenth-Century Literature* (Berkeley: University of California Press, 1972), p. 3.

29. *Ibid.*, p. 8.

30. *Ibid.*, pp. 24-25.

31. *Ibid.*, p. 155.

32. Richard Gelwick, *The Way of Discovery: An Introduction to the Thought of Michael Polanyi* (New York: Oxford University Press, 1977), p. 135.

33. Jonathan Edwards, as quoted in Clyde A. Holbrook, *The Ethics of Jonathan Edwards: Morality and Aesthetics* (Ann Arbor: University of Michigan Press, 1973), p. 185.

34. Paul L. Holmer, *C. S. Lewis: The Shape of His Faith and Thought* (New York: Harper & Row, 1976), p. 89.

35. Alan F. Blum, *Socrates: The Original and Its Images* (London: Routledge & Kegan Paul, 1978), p. 2.

36. Paul Ricoeur, *The Symbolism of Evil* (Boston: Beacon Press, 1969), pp. 347-357.

37. *Ibid.*, p. 351.

38. *Ibid.*, p. 352.

39. *Ibid.*, p. 349.

40. See H. Richard Niebuhr, *The Meaning of Revelation* (New York: Macmillan, 1941), pp. 80-96.

41. Hans-Georg Gadamer, "Man and Language," *Philosophical Hermeneutics*, trans. and ed. David E. Linge (Berkeley: University of California Press, 1976), p. 68.

42. David E. Linge, "Editor's Introduction," in Gadamer, *Philosophical Hermeneutics*, p. lv.

43. *Ibid.*

44. Arendt, *Thinking*, p. 98.

45. Gadamer, *Truth and Method*, p. 350.

46. See Anthony Giddens, *New Rules of Sociological Method: A Positive Critique of Interpretative Sociologies* (New York: Basic Books, 1976), pp. 155-162.

47. See Meagher, *Augustine*, pp. 1-28.

48. *Ibid.*, p. 292.

49. Edward H. Davidson, *Jonathan Edwards: The Narrative of a Puritan Mind* (Cambridge: Harvard University Press, 1968), p. 82.

3

Metaphysics of
Existence

The metaphysical question of why there is something rather
than nothing will not go away. The question is basic to our
existence—to our consciousness in relation to the cosmos.
Even to argue that there is no metaphysic of existence—or
that there is no need to speak of it—is a metaphysic on the
fundamental nature of being and our understanding of existence. The problem, then, is how to talk about and how to
believe in a metaphysic that is appropriate for our time.

Certainly we do not return to the older metaphysic, or we
cannot return with the same sensibility. The traditional metaphysic, incorporating the two-world theory of existence and
a language conceiving a personified God, is being severely
questioned. In a particular sense, metaphysics along with
theology and philosophy has reached an end. Not that God
has died (how could we ever know?), Hannah Arendt notes,
"but the way God has been thought of for thousands of years
is no longer convincing; if anything is dead, it can only be the
traditional *thought* of God."[1] Regarding metaphysics in general and the specific question of God, the old problems have
not disappeared; they refer to questions that are still meaningful. But the ways the questions are posed and answered
have lost their plausibility, and we are in search of a new
metaphysic of existence.

71

The Sacred and the Secular

Deeply embedded in our historical consciousness—and epistemology—is the division between the sacred and the secular. The terminology even provides a model of social development, suggesting the increasing "secularization" of modern society. The sacred and secular concepts have, of course, varying definitions and opposing meanings and usages. For example, the world has been divided into two separate realms, the secularity of "this world" and the sacredness of the "other world." A vastly different way of thinking about the sacred and the secular is to conceive of two qualities of existence, with the awe-filled character of the sacred informing the everyday secular pursuits of life. It is this conception, as opposed to the two-world notion, that I shall draw upon most heavily in a discussion of the developing metaphysic.

The classical two-world notion of the sacred and the secular has its grounding in the reality of social existence. In a period of the "bicameral mind," as Julian Jaynes calls it, prior to approximately 1200 B.C., there was a union of the body and mind with the divine.[2] Daily living was in complete association with the divine, the divine being part of the structure of the human nervous system. With the growth and complexity of society, and with cultural encounters, the human mind became conscious of itself, engaging in reflective and critical awareness. Language, metaphor, and reasoning now placed human beings in the world. The sacred and the secular, in other words, became divided. Contact with the divine is now very much a process of volition. There is the need for theology and philosophy—for a metaphysic—to make the elemental connections.

The complete integration of the sacred and the secular—where the two are one—is of a former time. The evolution of human consciousness gives primacy to the secular world, with only occasional reference to the sacred nature of existence.

This "desacralization," as Mircea Eliade calls it, prevades modern social existence, making it increasingly difficult to experience the sacred character of reality.[3] Nevertheless, every experience remains potentially sacred, just as every human experience is at the same time secular.

Human existence as both sacred and secular is dialectical, the sacred and the secular presenting two different realities of being in the world.[4] Without secular existence there could be no sacred existence, and without the sacred all life would be ordinary and shallow. The depth of reality is found in the dialectic of the sacred and the secular. Neither the sacred nor the secular can be experienced entirely independently of each other in modern times. The sacred without the secular would lose its meaning; the secular without the sacred would cease to allow a human existence. This holds, of course, until the time when the two become one in human consciousness and social existence—until there is a radical union of the worldly and the divine.

The most striking characteristic of the modern dialectic of the sacred and the secular is that no particular sphere of existence can be called sacred. The sacred as a complete transcendential experience is no longer accessible. The human being, Louis Dupré notes,

> no longer *directly* experiences the holy either in the world or in the mind. The outer world has become totally humanized. Nature is no longer perceived as filled with God's presence. It has become a field of operation in which function determines meaning. Nor does man discover the divine in the secret of his own heart.[5]

All human experiences now are a combination of the sacred and the secular. Modern existence is lived, however con-

sciously or unconsciously, within the tension and dialectic of
the sacred and the secular.

Even within the dialectic the difference between the sacred
and the secular is relative and varying. The predominance of
one over the other is always shifting from one situation to
another. One cannot exist without the other; one defines the
other: "There is no such thing as profaneness by itself."[6]
Every act and sign has something about it that both attests to
its secularity and protests against its profanity. All in life
shares in the sacred; all being is thereby impressed with the
touch of the holy.

The modernization of the sacred-secular dialectic has been
suggested in the Christian theology of Dietrich Bonhoeffer.
In rejecting the traditional metaphysic of the two worlds (the
divine world versus the profane world of everyday existence),
Bonhoeffer revised the theological conception of the sacred
and the secular. He describes the traditional division and its
limiting character: "The division of the total reality into a
sacred and a profane sphere, a Christian and a secular sphere,
creates the possibility of existence in a single one of these
spheres, a spiritual existence which has no part in secular
existence, and a secular existence which can claim autonomy
for itself and can exercise this right of autonomy in its
dealings with the spiritual sphere."[7]

Bonhoeffer argues that through the merging of the two
separate spheres of the sacred and the secular, the theological
aim of the Reformation is being fulfilled. Reality itself is
expanded by the integration into one sphere:

> There are not two realities, but only one reality, and
> that is the reality of God, which has become manifest in
> Christ in the reality of the world. Sharing in Christ we
> stand at once in both the reality of God and the reality
> of the world. The reality of Christ comprises the reality

of the world within itself. The world has no reality of its own, independently of the revelation of God in Christ.[8]

Rather than two spheres, standing side by side and competing with each other, there is the one sphere of a whole reality.

Although modern theology may call for a reality of one sphere—combining the sacred and the secular—and although in our own lives we actually combine the two spheres into one, in our philosophies and epistemologies we still tend to make the separation. We still prefer to divide human experience into two separate realms, reserving the secular for our everyday life and the sacred for special occasions. We conceive of two opposing ways of being in the world. While the distinction may serve an outdated psychology and sociology, it is not appropriate for what the postmodern experience is calling for. The sacred-secular distinction prevents us from understanding our human existence as lived in the reality of the whole world. The division of the world into the sacred and the secular finally prevents us from struggling for the transformation of a world that will make us whole, at one with the universe and grounded in all being.

A metaphysic of one world, integrating the sacred and the secular, must at the same time attend to the questions of time, history, and eternity. We continue to ask whether the final event in the evolution of the universe is within the present mode of time and history. Or will there be a time beyond history, the transhistorical that breaks out of the historical? Perhaps this last—the final eschatology—must remain a mystery. A metaphysic is not to answer all questions, but to raise our sense of awe and therein provide a home for us. Metaphysics is not a positivistic science. The unconditional remains in the world. The sacred permeates all areas of life and nature, not to be explained away by a science of the knowable. All that is known is also filled with mystery.

In the one world that is at once sacred and secular there is no place without mystery. All that is known, as the Catholic theologian Karl Rahner reminds us, is also filled with a mystery that is beyond explanation.[9] Mystery inheres in and is indispensable to our existence. The metaphysic of the sacred-within-secular and secular-within-sacred touches upon all subjects. In the unity is the mystery and the reality.

Traditional Metaphysics

In commonsense terms, without a conscious recognition of the sacred and the secular, the modern world has become secularized. The most obvious indication and representation of this secularization is the notion that "God is dead." Although there are signs of an increasing return to "God-talk," the trend of the last few decades has been toward a rejection of a metaphysic based on the idea of God. Two distinct but related processes are occurring in the course of secularization. On the one hand, the word "God" is being questioned; and on the other, the very existence of God (or whatever term can be used to represent a transcendental force) is in doubt. We are living in a time in which we find it difficult either to speak about God or to believe in that which God has always represented to us.

In theology, the metaphysical vision of God has been questioned seriously in the death-of-God theology.[10] However, the emphasis in most of this theology is not that God does not exist, but that our way of conceiving of what we have called God is in question. Bonhoeffer's lament on the passing of "religion as such," that our civilization has "come of age," is accompanied by the suggestion that "god is teaching us that we must live without him."[11] It is not God who has died, Bonhoeffer states, but it is with the suffering Christ that we live in the world. What we have called God, in other words, is now a living presence in the daily life of social existence.

The metaphysical problem that goes beyond any particular form of social existence—whether in the political economy of capitalism or in that of socialism—concerns the name and presence of God. The problem is a postmodern one, one that is especially important in the transformation from a capitalist to a socialist society. Capitalism can only be short term; it is based on class and competitive relations that cannot promote the values and ultimate concerns necessary for a true social existence. In the modern period, throughout the world, we have attempted the experiment of living without God, of trying to be in a world in which God is silent, of living without an idea of the infinite nature of being. The modern experience has been lived in the presence of God's absence— and the experiment has failed.

The problem can be resolved only in the struggle for social existence. A debate about metaphysics alone will not solve the problem. But it is also in our thinking and believing that we come to terms with the problems of our existence. Metaphysical questions in this sense are a fundamental part of daily life. At the center of metaphysics is the question of God, the question about the presence of anything beyond our finite selves and social reality, of anything that gives meaning to our existence. That question will not go away from either metaphysical discussion or our daily lives; it is ontological.

The question of the ultimate meaning of existence may not necessarily, of course, be posed in terms of the presence of a supreme God-being. A theistic metaphysic is but one of the ways of considering the problem. The traditional metaphysic is the theistic one: that there exists a God that is the creative source of the universe and that transcends the world yet is within it. Metaphysics in general is the search for ultimate meaning, and in the traditional metaphysic (as known particularly in the Judeo-Christian tradition) ultimate meaning is found in what is called God. To question or even reject the existence of a God—especially within the confines of a monotheistic, personified, male God figure—is not to reject the presence of a providential power in the universe. Another metaphysic of ultimate, supreme meaning may yet emerge in the postmodern period. Indeed, the new age may be recognized by the metaphysic that characterizes that age.

If some form of a language of God-talk persists, it will likely be with us in revised form. The metaphysic would refer to God, but there would be a new sensibility in the understanding and belief surrounding that metaphysic. The Christian existentialist John Macquarrie argues that "God" is the key word in theological metaphysics. God, accordingly, is the religious name for Being:

> The Being encountered is not an object of which we can talk in a disinterested way, but the Being in which we live and move and have our being. So too, religious discourse is always of God in his relation to us. When we talk of God, we talk at the same time of ourselves. The word "God" does not just signify Being, but also implies an evaluation of Being, a commitment to Being as Holy Being, Being that is gracious and judging.12

This is, certainly, the use of a God terminology in the modern existentialist philosophy of being. A problem arises when we consider the fact that in our philosophy (academic and everyday) we already may be seeking an alternative to existentialism. An existential metaphysic of God would also have to be revised.

The history of theology (existential and otherwise) has in recent decades tended either to withdraw from the world of everyday life or to become involved in it. Those theologians who have attempted to be more at home in the contemporary world have explained the notion of God in terms that would be more compatible in the modern world. For Tillich, God (in so far as Tillich is able to talk about God) is both transcendent and immanent. But God is not the name of a being that can be set alongside other beings. Rather, developing an existential theology, Tillich states that God is being-in-itself. God, then, is the *ground* of all being, the source of meaning erupting into everything that is finite, partial, and conditional. God is the name that we give to that which we care about most deeply. When we talk about God, notes Tillich, we are expressing our *ultimate concerns* about the meaning of our existence in the universe.[13]

Tillich is thus postulating a God above God, beyond rational categories and accepted in absolute faith. The theistic idea of God is to be transcended because, among other reasons, it is theologically wrong:

The God of theological theism is a being beside others and as such a part of the whole of reality. He certainly is considered its most important part, but as a part and therefore as subjected to the structure of the whole. He is supposed to be beyond the ontological elements and categories which constitute reality. But every statement subjects him to them. He is seen as a self which has a world, as an ego which is related to a thou, as a cause which is separated from its effect, as having a definite space and an endless time. He is a being, not being-itself. As such he is bound to the subject-object structure of reality, he is an object for us as subjects. At the same time we are objects for him as a subject. And this is decisive for the necessity of transcending theological theism. For God as a subject makes me into an object which is nothing more than an object. He deprives me of my subjectivity because he is all-powerful and all-

knowing. I revolt and try to make *him* into an object,
but the revolt fails and becomes desperate. God appears
as the invincible tyrant, the being in contrast with
whom all other beings are without freedom and subjectivity.[14]

That which we call God, beyond theism, can be spoken of
only in the symbols that are encountered in religious experience.

Following Tillich's theology, God is not to be rejected, as
in atheism, because one can no longer believe in God as a
personified being who has intentions as we know them. The
nature of God is discovered in the ultimate concerns of
human life. The meaning and purpose of life are to be found
within social existence. In other words, the sacred and the
secular are once again brought together.

Neither of them should be in separation from the other,
and both should realize that their very existence as
separated is an emergency, that both of them are rooted
in religion in the larger sense of the word, in the experience of ultimate concern. To the degree in which this is
realized the conflicts between the religious and the
secular are overcome, and religion has rediscovered its
true place in man's spiritual life, namely, in its depth,
out of which it gives substance, ultimate meaning, judgment, and creative courage to all functions of the
human spirit.[15]

Religion, as such, is the ground, the substance, and the depth
of our human social existence.

In addition to the existential critique of a theistic conception of God is the recent feminist critique of the male-
paternalistic image of God. The Judeo-Christian religions, in
particular, have been dominated for centuries by a male

monotheism. Such a conception of God can no longer be persausive for the postmodern consciousnes. Male monotheism has been viewed, historically and psychologically, as follows:

I think that male monotheism must be understood historically as a holding action in our long struggle to grow up: a step away from a magical-propitiatory relation to nature and toward self-responsibility for our condition. Jehovah, all-powerful though He was, did make binding covenants and sensible rules, and one could try arguing with Him. He was created single to represent unified, coherent natural and moral principles; parental because we still needed to feel externally protected and disciplined; and male because, on the deep mental levels tapped by religion, a father—so long as he is a figure whose presence in a prerational infancy was much less important than the mother's—is necessarily a more understandable, less magical authority: more of a fellow "I" to the human self in its ambivalent growth—across a lifetime and across millennia—toward autonomy. Implicit in that forward step was of course another, now in progress: to move beyond *all* supernatural parents.[16]

The identification of divinity with maleness, feminist theology notes, has easily led to male leadership within organized religion and to dominance of men in family and society. That this tradition was shaped more by historical circumstances than by divine providence is the message of feminist analysis.[17] In early Christianity, for example, with its gnostic influences, there was a feminine symbolism that applied, in particular, to God. Certain of the early texts describe God as a dyadic being containing both masculine and feminine, paternal and maternal, elements. There are other early texts in which a female God predominates. The decline of the feminine imagery of God occurred as Christianity carried out its missionary goals and adapted to the Greek and Roman cultures. Along the way, feminine religious symbolism was suppressed.

The sexism of our religious tradition is related, furthermore, to the dualistic and hierarchical mentality that Christianity inherited from the classical world. This dualism represents, Rosemary Radford Ruether shows, all the basic dualities: "the alienation of mind from the body; the alienation of the subjective self from the objective world; the subjective retreat of the individual, alienated from the social community; the domination or rejection of nature by spirit."[18] And the alienation of the masculine from the feminine is the primary sexual symbolism that characterizes all of these alienations. God the Father, beyond this world, is identified with the positive sides of these dualisms, and the irrational world of women, with its physicality and sensuality, is to be dominated. Through the centuries, Ruether writes, society "has in every way profoundly conditioned men and women to play out their lives and find their capacities within this basic antithesis."[19]

The dualism of the two worlds has influenced the theological conception of God as well. "When this dualistic pattern of thinking is combined with a symbolic tradition in which God is addressed and conceptualized in predominantly male language and imagery, the sexism of religious thinkers appears logical and consistent."[20] The language of existential theology is not exempt from this observation. As Valerie Saiving writes:

> It is clear that many of the characteristic emphases of contemporary theology—its definition of the human situation in terms of anxiety, estrangement, and the conflict between necessity and freedom; its identification of sin with pride, will-to-power, exploitation, self-assertiveness, and the treatment of others as objects

rather than persons; its conception of redemption as restoring to man what he fundamentally lacks (namely, sacrificial love, the I-Thou relationship, the primacy of the personal, and ultimately, peace)—it is clear that such an analysis of man's dilemma was profoundly responsive and relevant to the concrete facts of modern man's existence.[21]

Such a theology, implicitly male-centered or centered on typically masculine concerns, cannot speak to the particular spiritual and social concerns of women. As a theology develops around a revised imagery of God, it will also incorporate a nonsexist symbolism and a symbolism that expresses the ultimate needs and concerns of all in social existence.

It is with the realization that the crisis in contemporary society is as much spiritual as it is economic and political that we proceed with theological reflection. The task in our daily struggle and in our reflection is to create symbols that express our emerging sensibilities, experiences, and needs. The theologian Gordon D. Kaufman writes that "theologians should acknowledge much more openly how intuitively implausible the traditional theological concepts have become, and how much they are in need of radical reconstruction."[22] The central symbol of God, especially, has to be reconstructed so that it becomes significant for contemporary life. Whether we are theologians or engaged in life and reflection in other ways, the contemporary project is to reconstruct radically the central metaphysical notions by which we live and have our being. There is no alternative, as Kaufman reminds us: "The true human fulfillment to which the Christian community is devoted cannot be gained apart from the liberating and humanizing effects of theological and metaphysical self-consciousness and understanding."[23]

Through theological reflection—based necessarily on metaphysical assumptions—the deepest and most comprehensive

presuppositions of social existence are apprehended and articulated. The particular experiences of the present age are
confronted. Moreover, an essential objective in clarifying the
character of the age is that of "proposing new conceptual
formulations that would more adequately interpret experience for that time and place."[24] In going beyond the conventional wisdom of the period, theological reflection exposes
the structures of meaning and the patterns of thought and
action that underlie the social existence of the time. In this
respect, the reflection that is part of the struggle for social
existence raises human consciousness about the present condition and furthers human and social liberation. Again Kaufman notes: "All knowledge is for action; knowledge of the
ultimate presuppositions of our common life is to make
possible responsible action with respect to those presuppositions. This is what metaphysics is for."[25]

What form and content theological reflection will take is
being worked out in the daily struggle for social existence
and in the search for the meaning of social existence. The
appropriate meaning can be found only in the search and the
struggle. The traditional metaphysic will necessarily give way
to a reconstructed symbolism. As the Christian era—as we
have known it in a traditional metaphysic—is coming to an
end, a reconstructed metaphysic will be created to give meaning and direction to the new era.

In this reconstruction it may well be that the metaphysical
project itself will be altered. A newer and more appropriate
metaphysic will likely incorporate the notions indicated by
Heidegger, whereby our way of apprehending is drastically
changed.[26] In a newer metaphysic the emphasis will be on
meditative thinking rather than on objective calculation and
representation. The dualistic character of calculative thinking
that divides all things into subjects and objects will be surpassed by a holistic form of thought.

A reconstructed metaphysic will incorporate a symbolism of God that departs significantly from traditional symbolism. The traditional symbolism of God contains the classical duality of subject and object. Human beings, accordingly, are the subjects of an acting force beyond themselves, and human beings take God and "faith" in God as their object in the process of salvation. Such a metaphysic underlies both modern science (including technological dominance) and religion. Drawing from Heidegger's analysis of metaphysics, Carl L. Raschke notes that "without the achievement of subjective certitude, technology as the historical culmination of man's forgetfulness of Being for the sake of managing and controlling the items of his world would not have been possible."[27] A reconstructed metaphysic will have to go beyond the subject-object dualism that places human beings as the subjective arbiters of the universe.

Christianity has therefore been the precondition for modern secularity, being based on a metaphysic that divides all things in the universe into subjects and objects. The metaphysic of traditional theology is itself part of contemporary secularity: "Theology today stands as the living token of Nietzsche's prophecy that we have 'killed' God, inasmuch as it contrives its last defense by referring to the divine as an 'object' that can be re-presented and manipulated in accordance with the strictures of the experiencing subject, or the teleology of the will."[28]

The overcoming of the traditional metaphysic—in form and substance—demands a kind of reflection that is holistic instead of dualistic. A holistic metaphysic of the universe transcends the subject-object perspective of the symbolism in traditional metaphysics. The reconstruction of the world, of our social existence, in other words, is at the same time the reconstruction of metaphysics. Once again, we realize that theological reflection in our time requires a oneness with the

word. We must learn again to hear and to speak. As Thomas
Altizer observes:

> Theology today is most fundamentally in quest of a
> language and mode whereby it can speak. Above all it is
> in quest of a language whereby it can speak of God.
> Ever increasingly and decisively this quest is becoming a
> quest for language itself, and for a new language, a
> language whereby we can actually and fully speak.[29]

We listen in our struggle for the word to be spoken.

The traditional metaphysic no longer speaks the word to
us. Whether in the *form* of subject-object reflection or in the
substance of an anthropomorphic God, the old metaphysic is
in disarray. We seek a metaphysic that can be right for our
coming of age. We have not outgrown—nor shall we ever—our
need for symbols that are based on an underlying metaphysic. Because the old metaphysic is obsolete, a reconstructed metaphysic is necessary.

We cannot do without an essential symbolism, either in the
world of the past or in the postmodern age. There has to be a
symbolism—and a language appropriate to that symbolism—
to consider the kinds of questions that remain with us. The
fact that one of the most elementary questions of existence,
the question of death, remains with hardly a hint of a
language of reflection, indicates the poverty of our current
symbolism. Only a symbolism grounded in a reconstructed
metaphysic can begin to apprehend and to provide answers to
the questions of existence in the universe.

Our finitude begins to be grasped as we attend to matters
of the infinite. Finiteness is *in* the infinite, which we have
called God. How we concretely, in form and substance,
symbolize that which we call God is still the problem of a
reconstructed metaphysic. The infinite is grasped, however
tentatively, only in and through the world of social existence.

In the symbolic culture and in the structured reality of everyday life we come in contact with meaning in the universe.

The mystery of being is approached with all our doubt, but we ultimately seek meaning. Conversely and dialectically, in reflection and struggle we are left with the final ambiguity of the world. There is an ambiguity of existence that finally escapes any metaphysic. We are left ultimately with the fact that there is no place in existence where there is no mystery. The mystery is the life that inheres in all symbolism, and the mystery pervades the reconstruction of a metaphysic.

Religious Experience

The reconstruction of a metaphysic is necessitated by and made possible through religious experience. In the creation of a symbolic system we are able to experience that which is particular to being human—the religious; and in the religious we create the symbols that give meaning to our place in the universe. No matter how we try to exclude the religious from life, especially in modern times, the experience of being religious is basic to our human nature: "The human soul is so constructed as to require a religion, a doctrine about the meaning and center of life."[30] To regain the center of life is the objective in the reconstruction of a metaphysic in our time.

No matter how we try to compartmentalize our experiences, the religious is an integral part of human experience. The sacred, rather than being a separate realm of existence, is an experiencing of the religious within the world of everyday life. The symbols and structures that we construct are the meanings human beings make collectively in a combining of the sacred and the secular. All human experience is at once spiritual and material, sacred and secular.

Human culture, in other words, is religious. In the search
for meaning in the universe, culture is the constructed means
of symbolizing the meaning of social existence. Transcendence
through culture moves us not only into a symbolic world,
but transports us into the realm of infinite concern. Through
the culture of the world we reach out to that which remains
beyond definition, that which is beyond ourselves and our
concrete existence. Through culture we participate in the
ultimate, in the ground of our essential being. We attend to
the infinite, and are inspired by the unconditional.

The "theology of culture," as Tillich called it, recognizes
"that in every culture creation—a picture, a system, a law, a
political movement (however secular it may appear)—an ultimate concern in expressed, and that it is possible to recognize
the unconscious theological character of it."[31] Within every
cultural creation—including the substructure of the economic
order as well as the superstructure of ideas and social institutions—there is a spiritual expression. Given this concept of
the unity of the sacred and the profane, "there are no
persons, scriptures, communities, institutions, or actions that
are holy in themselves, nor are there any that are profane in
themselves. The profane can profess the quality of holiness,
and the holy does not cease to be profane."[32] The religious
substance of culture is manifest in all aspects of human
culture; every person is in some way related to the unconditional ground of being. The creation of human culture has
within it divine inspiration.

Through human social constructions, then, the transcendent is made possible. The transcendent—religious—
dimension is essential to being human, sometimes (and only
in relatively recent history) symbolized in the complex
notion of God. Whether or not the experience is symbolized
by an image of God, the transcendent is always with us. To

deny the transcendent is to take away from our quality of being human. Drawing from the mystical writings on the essential nature of transcendence, Dupré observes:

> The ultimate message of the mystic about the nature of selfhood is that the self is *essentially* more than a mere self, that transcendence belongs to its nature as much as the act through which it is immanent to itself, and that a total failure on the mind's part to realize this transcendence reduces the self to *less* than itself. The general trend of our civilization during the last centuries has not been favorable to that message. Its tendency has been to reduce the self to its most immediate and lowest common experiences. But for this restriction we pay the price of all-pervading feeling of unfulfillment and, indeed, of dehumanization. Deprived of its transcendent dimension, self-hood lacks the very space it needs for full self-realization.[33]

I would add that to the extent human culture attempts to exclude the transcendent, culture falls short of its real potential.

That the transcendent experience is fundamental to being human is shared by existential philosophy. Heidegger, although reluctant to be drawn into the debate of God, defines the essence of being human in terms of the holy. Questions of the divine can be posed only when we open ourselves to the holiness of our being.

> Only from the truth of Being can the essence of the holy be thought. Only from the essence of the holy is the essence of divinity to be thought. Only in light of the essence of divinity can it be thought or said what the word "God" is to signify.[34]

To exclude the holy from everyday life would be to deny the essence of our being human.

Social existence can truly be experienced only when apprehended with the dimension of the religious. When life is lived with the element of transcendance, the world is constructed and revealed in its fullest. The religious human being assumes a particular and characteristic mode of existence in the world. Eliade observes:

> Whatever the historical context in which he is placed, *homo religiosus* always believes that there is an absolute reality, *the sacred*, which transcends this world but manifests itself in this world, thereby sanctifying it and making it real. He further believes that life has a sacred origin and that human existence realizes all of its potentialities in proportion as it is religious—that is, participates in reality.[35]

The religious mode of being is in contrast to the life that is lived without a sense of the religious. To live without experiencing the religious is to accept a relativity of existence, even to deny the meaning of existence. This is the plight of much of modern existence.

> Modern nonreligious man assumes a new existential situation; he regards himself solely as the subject and agent of history, and he refuses all appeal to transcendence. In other words, he accepts no model for humanity outside the human condition as it can be seen in the various historical situations. Man *makes himself*, and he only makes himself completely in proportion as he desacralizes himself and the world. The sacred is the prime obstacle to his freedom. He will become himself only when he is totally demysticized. He will not be truly free until he has killed the last god.[36]

The modern human being and the modern culture, insofar as the religious element is excluded, assume a tragic existence—an aloneness in the universe, without meaning.

When the transcendent-sacred dimension is excluded, other myths are substituted. The secular societies of the present contain their own symbolic systems to deal with that which remains unknown and mysterious.[37] An eschatological hope of an absolute end to history, or the converse hope of the continual evolution of history, may temporarily satisfy the need for some sense of order and meaning. The redeeming role of "the chosen" may come to symbolize the course of social change. Finally, however, the existential crisis—the crisis of a solely secular existence—finds a resolution in the return to sacred concerns, in a joining of the sacred and the secular. The unity of the sacred and the secular is the paradigmatic solution for the crisis of social existence.

Thus, the crisis in the modern world is as much spiritual and religious as it is material. The reconstruction involves both a change in the political and economic realm and a change in the religious realm. Both reconstructions provide access to an essential existence. In other words, as the historian William G. McLoughlin argues, in our post-modern period we are experiencing (especially in the United States) a new "great awakening," the creation of new symbols and structures that will reconstitute the social and moral order.[38] The new reality combines the sacred and the secular; and in the process the religious experience becomes an integral part of everyday life in the world.

Symbols awaken in us the religious experience of being human—and being human collectively, in a common culture. The religious experience awakens in us, as well, the need and desire to create symbols that give meaning to our human and social existence. There would be no symbols—no word and no language—without religious experience.

Symbols, Metaphors, and Myths

The modern Western world, in both capitalist and socialist societies, represents the final stage of desacralization. The symbols that once were filled with religious experience now have little meaning. To attempt to live entirely within the secular and nonreligious realm is the modern experience. The symbols that remain to give meaning to our existence have only a remembrance of the sacred. The symbols by which we live, such as they are, are but substitutes for the symbols that were charged with the depth of meaning.

Thus, as Eliade observes, the secular existence of the human being in modern societies "is still nourished and aided by the activity of his unconscious, yet without thereby attaining to a properly religious experience and vision of the world."[39] The substance of a former religious symbolism is now relegated to the unconscious, nevertheless offering occasional solutions to the difficulties of life, playing the role of religion. Eliade, drawing from Christian symbolism, likens the modern condition to the "fall," a second fall that has followed the separation of the world into two spheres, the sacred and the secular:

From the Christian point of view, it could also be said that nonreligion is equivalent to a new "fall" of man—in other words, that nonreligious man has lost the capacity to live religion consciously, and hence to understand and assume it; but that, in his deepest being, he still retains a memory of it, as, after the first "fall," his ancestor, the primordial man, retained intelligence enough to enable him to rediscover the traces of God that are visible in the world. After the first "fall," the religious sense descended to the level of the "divided consciousness"; now, after the second, it has fallen even

further, into the depths of the unconscious; it has been
"forgotten."[40]

Modern symbols, until they join holistically the sacred and
the secular, attempt to provide whatever meaning they can,
as limiting and unfulfilling as that meaning may be.

That we continue to live daily with and through symbols is
obvious. But that we are in the process, in our own time, of
creating symbols for a new world is the point that I am
making. Reconstructed social forms and institutions will be
developed, relating to symbols that are appropriate for our
age. At the moment we are playing out in our hearts and
minds, through the construction of symbols, the creation of a
new social existence.

The creation of symbols, then, is a fundamental process in
the construction of a new social world. The movement to a
postmodern world involves a paradigm change that is perva-
sive. Creation of a new world, charged with religious symbolism, not unlike the formation of the social world of early
Christianity, is described by John Gager as follows:

Old symbols are given new meaning and new symbols
come to life; new communities define themselves in
opposition to previous traditions; a new order of the
sacred is brought into being and perceived by the community as the source of all power and meaning; new
rituals emerge to remind the community of this sacred
order by creating it anew in the act of ritual celebration;
mechanisms are established for preserving this new
world and for adapting it to changing circumstances;
and eventually an integrated world view may emerge,
including systems of theology, sacred scriptures, and
ecclesiastical offices whose task is to give meaning not
just to the community itself but to all other worlds as
well.[41]

I am arguing that we are currently engaged in the creation of new symbols and the reconstruction of old ones in the transformation of our social existence.

This is not to assume that we shall return to the symbolisms of the sacred in accordance with their original meaning. Through reinterpretation we can communicate with the sacred; but by making known the prior understanding we are able to bring a new sense of the sacred to the secular aspect of existence. In the process of interpretation and the recreation of symbols, the old sacred-versus-secular symbolization is "demythologized."[42] The hidden dimension of the symbol is brought to light, and in the reconstruction the sacred element is united with the secular on a new level. Social existence is recharged and revitalized in the reconstruction of symbols.

In the reconstruction of symbols we are attempting to give meaning to our experience, and to our ever-changing experiences. Symbols, removed from direct perception and experience, order and organize our perceptions and experiences, making both possible. For example, a construction such as *world*, Kaufman suggests, "is never an object of direct perception; it is, rather, a concept with which we hold together in a unified totality all our experience and knowledge of objects—everything having its own proper place 'within' the world."[43] Likewise, the symbol of *God* cannot be properly understood as an object of direct experience or as an objective reality. "To regard God as some kind of describable or knowable object over against us would be at once a degradation of God and a serious category error."[44] We are continually reshaping and remaking our symbols, including the symbol of God, to give meaning to the new experiences of our existence.

Symbols, which order yet are removed from experience, form a paradigm in which the complexity of experience can be grasped. Symbols are *metaphors*. The whole within which all experience and reality can be comprehended is constructed in terms of likeness and comparison. One idea or thing is used to denote another, to suggest a likeness between ideas or things; thus, "God is *like*. . . ." The symbol as metaphor is a construction of the mind on the basis of experience, but a construction for which there is reference to a complex of ideas or events on another level. The language and symbol of the metaphor abstracts from concrete experience and thereby orders experience—all in comparison or contrast to something else. The empirical experience is understood in terms of another idea or thing, moving dialectically between two different levels of abstraction.

Hence, our concrete experiences are understood in terms of a higher-order conception. In particular, and ultimately, experience is given meaning in comparison to a metaphysical concept. A metaphysic, then, allows us to order and interpret the actual facts of experience in a convincing way. On the metaphysical nature of the metaphor, Kaufman notes: "The metaphysical task is most fundamentally the constructive and imaginative one of creating an overarching conception of reality or the world within which all the dimensions and elements of experience can be seen, both in their unique individuality and in their interdependence and interconnection with each other."[45] The metaphysical metaphor is the most powerful—and religious—instrument for bringing meaning into our human and social existence. It is human imagination at its ultimate.

We live, and we live ultimately, in metaphor. Our particular culture, as with all cultures, is grounded in metaphors, metaphors that are of metaphysical import. Our vision of reality is understood through and given meaning in metaphor. However, our metaphors are not simply decorative substitutes for what is otherwise "real." Metaphors, as used theologically and religiously, are rather a form of life in themselves; they are a way of redescribing reality according to its true essence for a particular social existence.

The metaphor provides and provokes tension between the symbol of the metaphor and the concrete experience.[46] The metaphor can disorient us, so that we may reorient ourselves in the consideration of another possibility of action, belief, and existence. The New Testament parables serve this purpose most classically. David Tracy comments on the parables of the prodigal son and the vineyard:

> Recall the father's extravagant feast for the irresponsible returned prodigal and the relative lack of celebration the father accords the responsible elder son. In the vineyard parable, recall the extravagance—and seeming flouting of simple justice—in the way the employer pays the laborers who were hired late in the day the same wage as those who labored all day. These extravagant actions in these realistic narratives are, in fact, disorienting to the reader. Yet that strategy of disorientation may serve the function of reorienting the reader by disclosing a new religious possibility; a way of being-in-the-world not based on the ethics of justice and merit but of pure gift, pure graciousness, indeed, in Wesley's famous phrase, of "pure unbounded love."[47]

Whether in Biblical parables or contemporary tales, we are awakened to the possibility of social existence. In metaphor we come to know the word.

The metaphor, expressed in language, bridges the gap between everyday experience and the invisible world of value and meaning. Speaking through metaphors we attach the meaning denoted in the metaphor to concrete appearances. Meaning is now visible, given appearance in everyday life. Metaphors, Arendt reminds us, "are the threads by which the mind holds on to the world even when, absentmindedly, it has lost direct contact with it, and they guarantee the unity of human experience." She continues: "In the thinking process itself they serve as models to give us our bearings lest we stagger blindly among experiences that our bodily senses with their relative certainty of knowledge cannot guide us through."[48] Through metaphor the world becomes one, uniting experience and meaning.

The world of everyday experience is known to us and is given meaning through the symbols that are inherent in the metaphor. In one version or another—expressed sacredly or secularly, or sometimes combined—the symbols within the metaphor are presented in narrative form. Our world is thereby known to us through *myth*. The myths of a culture place the symbols in relation to and in a tension with one another. That complex whole which is signified by myth may be in the form of a drama, a narration of events, personages, and history.[49] The drama of the myth regains some of the unity of spirit and matter, where myth and experience are once again one. Myths are most relevant for the reconstruction of social existence, in moving beyond the modern age.

In the reconstruction of the social and moral order, the substance of the symbols, metaphors, and myths is critical. The argument is not for the seriousness of symbols, metaphors, and myths (their seriousness is already assumed), but for the character of their particular content. In our own case, in the crisis of advanced capitalism in the United States, the substance of our constructions can either aid the crisis—in further supporting the capitalist system—or they can allow us to move to another social existence. One writer in liberation theology asks, in particular, about the role of Christian symbols:

What function will the Christian symbols serve during this period of critical and grave crisis in U.S. capitalism?

Will they serve to diffuse the focus, to legitimate the call
for austerity and social discipline, to help people adjust
to the attack on working people and their families and
on the life of the poor? In short, will the symbols serve
to accommodate the crisis? *Or* will they serve in an
effort to challenge, unmask and unravel once and for all
the dream that is fundamentally flawed as a human
dream because of its basis and foundation in the rights
of property over people?[50]

The reconstruction of social existence requires the reconstruction of our symbols as well. The struggle for a new
society takes place as the symbols for human possibility are
recreated. Social existence cannot be reconstructed without a
recreation of the cultural imagination.

The contemporary transformation in social existence is
occurring with the symbolism of the prophetic tradition. Our
destiny, as Tillich has reminded us, is directed by the powers
of our origin.[51] And in the Marxian analysis of capitalist
society, the presupposition of providence receives concrete
application: that capitalism is in the process of being transformed into socialism. It is in the socialist principle, in our
recognition of providence in a religious socialism, that we
integrate the past, present, and future. A bond is formed
between origin and a transcendence to the goal of socialism.

A religious socialism necessarily rejects the narrow materialist doctrine of Marxism. It radicalizes Marxism "by shed-
ding those elements of Marxism which are derived from
bourgeois materialism or idealism."[52] Religious socialism
thus seeks a basis that lies beyond the opposition between
the materialistic and the idealistic conceptions of human and
social life. It has a dual starting point: "namely, the *unity of
that which is vital and spiritual* in man, and the simultaneous
disruption of that unity which is the source of the threat to
man's being."[53] The meaning of existence must incorporate

both the material and the spiritual world. With this conception, in the struggle *against* demonized society and *for* a meaningful society, religious socialism discerns a necessary expression for the expectation of infinite being.

It is in the principle, the symbol, of socialism that this expectation is found. As a principle, a dynamic concept that "contains the possibility of making understandable new and unexpected realizations of a historical origin," socialism stands in a critical relation to reality.[54] It allows us to assess our situation and to transcend it in terms that are yet to be developed. The socialist principle is not a general demand standing over history, but neither is it merely the description of a unique historical phenomenon:

> Rather it is a particular principle that at the same time expresses human being in general. It is rooted in a primordial human element: the demand, the transcendent, the expectation of the new. This is its universality. It has been formed historically in the development of the Judeo-Christian tradition, down to the Christian humanism of bourgeois society; and it has come to specific realization in the Western proletariat. The universal and the particular elements—human being (*Sein*) and proletarian existence (*Dasein*)—therefore do not stand alongside each other in an unrelated way. They are related through a history that reaches back to the origins of life, and which leads via Christianity and humanism to socialism.[55]

The universal element of socialism is currently being worked out in the particular historical struggle in capitalist society, but will find new expression in a yet unperceived form.

The problem that socialism faces is breaking out of its origins in capitalism. This is its inner conflict, between origin and goal. The orthodox (secular) socialist interpretation of

human nature and society is bound by its origins in a bourgeois humanism that cuts us ,off from the transcendent.
Human life, accordingly, is to be realized only in ourselves;
the meaning of life is to be found in a conditional, finite
fulfillment. Even in the collectivity of social life, we are left
to face our loneliness and emptiness as autonomous beings,
necessarily separated from the spiritual side of our being.
Religion, if allowed into the scheme of things, is merely a
private matter, not an integral part of the community. The
strategy is misplaced: "To make religion a private matter
means to exclude it from the arena of political struggles, and
to turn it over to the individual or to a free association of
individuals."[56]

Hence, it is in the religious dimension of socialism that
there is the hope and possibility of truly transforming human
society. There must be an ultimate concern about being, a
place for the unconditional in our thought and action. This is
to replace the void in contemporary socialism, a void based
on a narrowly constructed scientific and technical, deter-
ministic and antireligious, orthodox Marxism. Without a
genuinely religious and transcendent dimension, only an
earthly and this-worldly fulfillment can be hoped for sometime in the future; and even that is in certain danger of being
coopted in the struggle against capitalism when pursued without the element of the spiritual. If a despiritualized socialism
is ever established, "without the acceptance of a religious
foundation and the symbols expressing it, no system of a
planned society can escape a speedy self-destruction."[57] A
religious socialist society, when achieved, is one in which the
class struggle has been replaced not only by a classless society
but also by a social unity (a "sacramental community") in
which human activity has meaning in an ultimate as well as
temporal sense.

We are thus to be transformed, immanently to transcend
the finitudes of the spirit of capitalism; this is the socialist

expectation. The prophetic attitude is essential to religious socialism: "Both prophetic and socialist expectation are a witness of life to its fundamental openness. They are a protest of life against false concepts of transcendence that inevitably call forth, in opposition, false concepts of immanence."[58] Here is an eschatology working through history, but shattering and changing it.

The socialist struggle, therefore, requires categories and symbols that speak to the fundamental question of both material existence and sacred essence. Marxism provides a language for the former (material existence) and a conception of the possibilities of a secular, humanistic essence. It includes the prophetic notion of redemption through a this-worldly socialist society. Marxism, however, fails to provide us with the symbols that relate to questions of the infinite and eternal that we apprehend in our lives. The socialist principle has to address the fullness of our being, responding to our most fundamental needs (spiritual as well as material). Religious symbolism is necessary in all aspects of social and cultural life, in revolution as in everyday living.

The socialist expectation is for the time filled with unconditioned meaning in a meaningful social order. That moment of time is signified by the symbol *kairos*, the prophetic realized through the principle of socialism.

Kairos is the fulfilled moment of time in which the present and the future, the holy that is given and the holy that is demanded meet, and from whose concrete tensions the new creation proceeds in which sacred import is realized in necessary form. Prophetism is consciousness of Kairos in the sense of the words: "Repent; the time *(kairos)* is fulfilled and the kingdom of God is at hand." Thus the sacramental and the critical attitudes are united in the consciousness of the Kairos, in the spirit of prophetism.[59]

The new being—the redeeming creative power in reality—
appears at the moment of the reunion of spirit and matter. A
reconcilation with the ultimate, the unconditional. Such is
the symbolism that will bring the metaphysical to the struggle for social existence.

Metaphysics in the World

The message is that metaphysics is a part of the real world.
The particular metaphysic that we know in our time and
place is an expression of the cultural and historical situation.
Metaphysics, rather than merely an abstract speculation
within theology and philosophy, is a force in the transformation of historical existence. In other words, the metaphysical
as it takes root within actual social and cultural life is an
integral part of the world.[60] A metaphysic does not refer to a
reality apart from the world of concrete experience, as pos-
tulated by the two-world theory of reality, but is within the
one world that we know and move and have our being.

The argument is that metaphysics has to be restored consciously to our lives in the fullness of our social existence.
Social theory about the nature of our existence cannot be
devoid of the metaphysical. Otherwise, the descriptions and
the prescriptions that follow from that theory will deny the
true nature of existence. The commonsense theories of our
existence related to or following from social theory must
incorporate a metaphysic that gives meaning to our existence.
If the Christian era is coming to an end, with an ending of its
particular metaphysic, then a new metaphysic must surely
come to take its place. A metaphysic of transformation in
this world, consistent with the word that unfolds in the

universe, is the metaphysic that is giving meaning and substance to the postmodern period.

The metaphysic as found in socialist theory and practice, especially in Marxism, is part of an emerging metaphysic. The historical process is viewed (drawing from the Judeo-Christian tradition) as moving in a providential direction—moving to the fullest potential of human history in the world.[61] The better world is to be achieved in a kingdom on earth. The transformation is a process of revelation. This is a metaphysic that is not removed from the world, but is known and takes place in the world.

To be overcome, however, is a metaphysic that solely emphasizes a secular and material existence, to the exclusion of the transcendent. The two-world theory of reality has easily and conveniently separated material life from spiritual life. In dividing the world into secular and sacred spheres, human beings have had the apparent choice of selecting different realms for different situations in everyday life, thus segmenting their lives. A holistic metaphysic, in sharp contrast, provides the possibility of bringing material and spiritual existence together. The material would not be pursued without the spiritual, and the spiritual would be grounded in everyday reality. The ultimate is found neither in some "other" world nor in a completely material existence, but at the point where a metaphysic is realized in the world. To use a symbol: God is on earth and the earth is in the divine universe.

The metaphysical can be constructed and understood only in terms of the world; and the world can be truly comprehended only in terms of ultimate-metaphysical consideration. Metaphysics appears in the process of struggling for social existence and in reflection about the meaning of that exis-

tence. The metaphysical, whether of God or another symbol,
is not above reality, but is within reality. André Dumas,
discussing Bonhoeffer's theological ontology in Christian
terms, states a one-world metaphysic that is able

> to speak of God not *above* reality, but at the point of
> his hidden presence *in* reality, remembering that the
> incarnation is the one place where the Christian can
> understand God's transcendence, and that as a result
> such transcendence does not create a Plantonic division
> between earthly appearances and heavenly essences, but
> that it establishes, in this world, the upholding of a
> claim that structures its own reality.[62]

Whatever the appropriate symbolism for the word of the
universe, we are speaking about metaphysical involvement *in*
the world.

A reconstructed metaphysic is a turning toward the world
rather than a turning away from it. That which we call God is
not beyond the world but within it. A metaphysic that turns
us away from the world (often in the name of "religion") is
no longer appropriate for the social existence that is in the
process of postmodern transformation. The word in the universe is known only in our everyday, historical existence—in
the words of human speech. As Bonhoeffer has written, "A
glimpse of eternity is revealed only through the depths of our
earth, only through the storms of a human conscience."[63] We
understand not in leaving the world but in our struggles
within it.

The metaphysics of existence, thus, is of the world rather
than separate from it. That metaphysics has become either
separated from existence (as in Platonism and most of Christianity) or almost completely *hidden* from the world (as in
modern times) is only a temporary condition. In the recon-

struction of social existence, we are reconstructing a metaphysic that will allow us once again to be truly in the world, apprehending at the same time the eternal meaning of the universe. Our faith is found in the creation of a metaphysic for social existence.

NOTES

1. Hannah Arendt, *Thinking* (New York: Harcourt Brace Jovanovich, 1978), p. 10.

2. Julian Jaynes, *The Origin of Consciousness and the Breakdown of the Bicameral Mind* (Boston: Houghton Mifflin, 1976).

3. Mircea Eliade, *The Sacred and the Profane: The Nature of Religion*, trans. Willard R. Trask (New York: Harcourt Brace Jovanovich, 1959), p. 3.

4. See Louis Dupré, *The Other Dimension: A Search for the Meaning of Religious Attitudes* (Garden City: Doubleday, 1972), pp. 14-17.

5. *Ibid.*, p. 23.

6. Hans-Georg Gadamer, *Truth and Method* (New York: Seabury Press, 1975), p. 133.

7. Dietrich Bonhoeffer, *Ethics*, ed. Eberhard Bethge (New York: Macmillan, 1955), p. 196.

8. *Ibid.*, p. 197.

9. See Karl Rahner, *Foundations of Christian Faith. An Introduction to the Idea of Christianity*, trans. William V. Dych (New York: Seabury Press, 1978), pp. 44-89.

10. See, in particular, John A.T. Robinson, *Honest to God* (Philadelphia: Westminster Press, 1963).

11. Dietrich Bonhoeffer, *Letters and Papers from Prison*, ed. Eberhard Bethge (New York: Macmillan, 1966), p. 219.

12. John Macquarrie, *God-Talk: An Examination of the Language and Logic of Theology* (New York: Harper & Row, 1967), p. 101.

13. See Paul Tillich, *Systematic Theology*, Vol. 1 (Chicago: University of Chicago Press, 1951), passim.

14. Paul Tillich, *The Courage to Be* (New Haven: Yale University Press, 1952), pp. 184-185.

15. Paul Tillich, *Theology of Culture*, ed. Robert C. Kimball (New York: Oxford University Press, 1959), p. 19.

16. Dorothy Dinnerstein, "The Uses of Gender," *New York Times Book Review*, July 29, 1979, pp. 10-11.

17. Elaine H. Pagels, "What Became of God the Mother? Conflicting Images of God in Early Christianity," in Carol P. Christ and Judith Plaskow (eds.) *Womanspirit Rising: A Feminist Reader in Religion* (New York: Harper & Row, 1979), pp. 107-119.

18. Rosemary Radford Ruether, "Motherearth and the Megamachine: A Theology of Liberation in a Feminine, Somatic and Ecological Perspective," *ibid.*, p. 44.

19. *Ibid.*

20. Carol P. Christ and Judith Plaskow, "Introduction: Womanspirit Rising," *ibid.*, p. 5.

21. Valerie Saiving, "The Human Situation: A Feminine View," *ibid.*, p. 35.

22. Gordon D. Kaufman, "Metaphysics and Theology," *Cross Currents*, 28 (Fall 1978), p. 340.

23. *Ibid.*

24. *Ibid.*, p. 336.

25. *Ibid.*, p. 337.

26. See Carl A. Raschke, "The End of Theology," *Journal of the American Academy of Religion*, 46 (June 1978), pp. 159-179.

27. *Ibid.*, p. 166.

28. *Ibid.*, p. 170.

29. Thomas J.J. Altizer, *The Self-Embodiment of God* (New York: Harper & Row, 1977), p. 1.

30. Eduard Heimann, "Tillich's Doctrine of Religious Socialism," in Charles W. Kegley and Robert W. Bretall (eds.), *The Theology of Paul Tillich* (New York: Macmillan, 1952), p. 318.

31. Tillich, *Theology of Culture*, p. 27.

32. Paul Tillich, *On the Boundary: An Autobiographical Sketch* (New York: Scribner, 1966), p. 71.

33. Louis Dupré, *Transcendent Selfhood: The Loss and Rediscovery of the Inner Life* (New York: Seabury Press, 1976), p. 104.

34. Martin Heidegger, "Letter on Humanism," *Basic Writings*, ed. David Farrell Krell (New York: Harper & Row, 1977), p. 230.

35. Eliade, *The Sacred and the Profane*, p. 202.

36. *Ibid.*, p. 203.

37. See *ibid.*, pp. 205-210.

38. William G. McLoughlin, *Revivals, Awakenings, and Reform: An Essay on Religion and Social Change in America, 1607-1977* (Chicago: University of Chicago Press, 1978), pp. 179-216.

39. Eliade, *The Sacred and the Profane*, p. 212.

40. *Ibid.*, p. 213.

41. John G. Gager, *Kingdom and Community: The Social World of Early Christianity* (Englewood Cliffs: Prentice-Hall, 1975), p. 11.

42. On "demythologization," see Paul Ricoeur, *The Symbolism of Evil*, trans. Emerson Buchanan (Boston: Beacon Press, 1969), pp. 352-353.

43. Kaufman, "Metaphysics and Theology," p. 328.

44. *Ibid.*, p. 329.

45. *Ibid.*, p. 332.

46. On the emerging notion of tension and interaction in New Testament hermeneutics, see Paul Ricoeur, *The Rule of Metaphor: Multi-Disciplinary Studies of the Creation of Meaning in Language*, trans. Robert Czerny (Toronto: University of Toronto Press, 1977).

47. David Tracy, "Metaphor and Religion: The Test Case of Christian Texts," *Critical Inquiry*, 5 (Autumn 1978), p. 100.

48. Arendt, *Thinking*, p. 109.

49. Ricoeur, *Symbolism of Evil*, pp. 164-171.

50. Kathleen Schultz, "Symbols of Struggle: Unmasking the Dream," in *Is Liberation Theology for North America?* (New York: Theology in the Americas, 1978), p. 111.

51. Paul Tillich, *The Socialist Decision*, trans. Franklin Sherman (New York: Harper & Row, 1977), p. 108.

52. Paul Tillich, *Political Expectation* (New York: Harper & Row, 1971), p. 46.

53. *Ibid.*, pp. 46-47.

54. Tillich, *Socialist Decision*, p. 9.

55. *Ibid.*, p. 64.

56. *Ibid.*, p. 80.

57. Paul Tillich, "Man and Society in Religious Socialism," *Christianity and Society*, 8 (Fall 1943), p. 10.

58. Tillich, *Socialist Decision*, p. 111.

59. Tillich, *Political Expectation*, p. 61.

60. See Kaufman, "Metaphysics and Theology," pp. 338-339.

61. See the discussion in Gerard Raulet, "Critique of Religion and Religion as Critique: The Secularized Hope of Ernst Bloch," *New German Critique*, 9 (Fall 1978), pp. 71-85. On the metaphysic in

Marxism, see Arend Theodoor van Leeuwen, *Critique of Heaven* (New York: Scribner, 1972).

62. André Dumas, *Dietrich Bonhoeffer: Theologian of Reality* (New York: Macmillan, 1971), p. 114.

63. Dietrich Bonhoeffer, *No Rusty Swords* (New York: Harper & Row, 1965), p. 47.

4

Critical Meaning
of Social Existence

The search for meaning in the world is at the same time the reconstruction of the world. That the conventional meaning of the age, or the lack of meaning, is inappropriate for the reconstruction is our starting point. That meaning is metaphysically grounded as well as anchored in concrete experience is our underlying assumption. A critical understanding of existence is rooted in the depth of reality.

The commonsense philosophy that gives meaning to the contemporary period is some version of existentialism. The contemporary sensibility shares in the twentieth-century philosophical movement that takes a subjective view of the individual negotiating life in the existentials of the "human condition." In other words, the commonsense philosophy, whether practiced in the academy or in everyday life, is based on an individualistic psychology of existence. The individual being is seen as groping in the world for meaning, often estranged from the "authentic" self, and trying to regain some sense of selfhood in an atomistic world of fellow beings. When the social nature of existence is considered, it is generally regarded as the sum total of individual actions, as the residual of being human.

The individualistic symbolism of human existence, I am arguing, is inappropriate for the reconstruction of social existence. Although we may attempt to hold to the existential interpretation of being personally human, existentialism will have to be elevated to the realm of the social and the cultural. The meaning of existence must be understood in terms of a symbolism that is based on *social existence*. The reconstruction that is taking place critically interprets the world according to the meaning of the existence that is social. The reconstruction moves us beyond individualism in life (and the related individualistic psychology) to an existence that recognizes and fulfills our social being—our social existence in the world. A symbolism, metaphysically grounded, is emerging that develops the meaning of social existence. It is a symbolism that allows us continually to transform our social existence.

Social Existence

Contemporary culture incorporates a symbolism that stresses the extremes of two important dimensions of social existence. In his book *Beyond Existentialism and Zen*, George Rupp, placing the issue in theological terms, outlines the two dimensions as follows:

> The first is the question of whether salvation as the goal of the religious life is an individual or a communal and ultimately universal affair. The second is the question of whether historical existence is of intrinsic value or only of instrumental worth as a means to a finally super-historical end.[1]

Our twentieth-century culture tends, applying Rupp's terms, to emphasize individual salvation and the intrinsic value of the historical present. What our culture tends to exclude is the communal or social meaning of existence and the trans-historical meaning of the present. But we need not conceptualize the present as all-important *or* as only instrumentally important; rather, it is important in its own right because of its transhistorical significance. Similarly, our lives are of significance religiously and socially in the construction of a world of universal import. Temporal social existence is the only means and end in the full realization of the universal social kingdom.

Another way of approaching a conceptualization of social existence is according to the notion of "limiting" situations or conditions in being human.[2] As I noted in the last chapter, the presence of an ultimate concern and the need for religious experience, as essentially expressed in symbols, metaphors, and myths, are fundamental matters to our being human. These matters are limiting conditions in our existence. Existentialists and phenomenologists have referred to other limiting conditions, particularly to the conditions of guilt, anxiety, and death. Likewise, there are the "positive" limiting experiences, such as creativity, joy, and trust. If these experiences and conditions are limits to being human, they are also, in a phenomenological understanding, the essential aspects of being human.

Let us assume, then, that there are fundamental conditions to being human. But this is not to assume that these are primarily of individual significance. I am arguing that what could otherwise be interpreted as a basic individual psychology is primarily of social significance. Let us consider the grandest and most awesome of all the limiting conditions, that of *death*, as described most persuasively by Ernest Becker in his book, *The Denial of Death*. The problem begins with the aloneness of the individual in the universe, with the terror of our own bodies in relation to everything beyond—our "experiential burden":

Man's body is a *problem* to him that has to be explained. Not only his body is strange, but also its inner

landscape, the memories and dreams. Man's very in-
sides—his self—are foreign to him. He doesn't know who
he is, why he was born, what he is doing on the planet,
what he is supposed to do, what he can expect. His own
existence is incomprehensible to him, a miracle just like
the rest of creation, closer to him, right near his pound-
ing heart, but for that reason all the more strange. Each
thing is a problem, and man can shut out nothing.[3]

Becker suggests that the human being must deal with the
terror of being human, of life and death, of being and
nonbeing, by *repressing* the terror of being human. "The
great boon of repression is that it makes it possible to live
decisively in an overwhelmingly miraculous and incomprehensible world, a world so full of beauty, majesty, and terror
that if animals perceived it all they would be paralyzed to
act."[4] Individually, in these terms, we lie to ourselves, we
escape from our own creatureliness. The solution is mainly
private, individual in form. Each person carries out his or her
own repression in order to keep from going mad. Becker also
assumes that because we do not have an innate authority over
the self, depending instead on the authority of others, we
cannot be at home in the world.

Reality is faced, for Becker, by repression and the lie, but
with the aid of an ultimate value attached to life. The
ultimate appeal is to religion. We desire to belong:

It seems that the yielding element in heroic belonging-
ness is inherent in the life force itself, one of the truly
sublime mysteries of created life. It seems that the life
force reaches naturally even beyond the earth itself,
which is one reason why man has always placed God in
the heavens.[5]

A religious culture is created to deny human creatureliness. Life is thereby given meaning, in the commitment that is also, for Becker, a necessary escape.

My purpose is not to denigrate the importance Becker places on death or to deny the importance of religion in coming to terms with being human. What I am stressing is that all of these conditions can be recognized, but recognized within the conceptualization of social existence. Religion is more a positive *social* force than an individualistic and negative response to terror. We do not so much repress our fear of death—through cultural symbols and mechanisms—but, rather, construct a culture as social beings to realize our social being. We are "beholden to others" not because we lack individual autonomy but because we are social beings from the beginning. Religious-spiritual experience comes out of our social existence, not out of individual repression.

The existentialist style of philosophizing, as Macquarrie calls it, is centered for the most part on the individual and the personal solutions to the problems of existence. From the standpoint of an analysis of social existence, this is the definite limitation of existentialism: "Probably all the leading existentialists pay at least lip-service to the truth that man exists as a person only in a community of persons. But in the main they are concerned with the individual whose quest for authentic selfhood focuses on the meaning of personal being."[6] Existentialists may show that interpersonal relations are at an inauthentic level, often recommending individualism as a revolt against this inauthenticity. Such analysis does not usually, however, delineate the shape of an authentic "being-with-others."

When existentialists do break out of a narrow individualism, they focus on the interpersonal, suggesting a theory of intersubjectivity. The interpersonal relations they investigate still tend to be on the intimate and domestic level rather than on the intergroup or societal level.[7] Because the individual is taken as the starting point in existentialism, the analysis retains an emphasis on the existence of the individual.

A social analysis—but nevertheless a restricted social analysis—is evident in the work of one of the most socially oriented existentialists, Gabriel Marcel. As a religious existentialist, Marcel considers the transcendental aspects of human life, in which the human being reaches out to others in a way that moves the person closer to others and to God. A commentator observes the following about Marcel's existentialism, in comparison to Heidegger's:

> For Heidegger man struggles against enormous difficulties to find *himself*—free, at last, of all the falsity around and inside him; whereas for Marcel man only finds himself through solidarity with others, through the "actualization" of his freedom in several kinds of love: a wife, a husband, friends, the person one may meet only briefly, but in a way that is honorable and kind-spirited on both sides—without false or automatic gestures.[8]

The person is actualized, accordingly, with others and through ultimate transcendence.

Certainly Marcel moves a step beyond the extreme individualism of most other versions of existentialism. He has a social concern, however limited, stating in his *The Mystery of Being* that "the more my existence takes on the character of including others, the narrower becomes the gap which separates it from being; the more, in other words, I am."[9] He builds solidly into his existentialist notions about the fellowship of being, love for others, and participation in being. It is only in the participation with others in the world that there is human being; participation is the foundation for the experience of existence.[10] Finally, his philosophy embodies an essentialism that goes beyond existentialism. Marcel suggests an existentialism that transcends itself, going beyond materialism, opening "itself out to the experience of the suprahuman."[11] What remains, however, is the need for recognizing social existence on its own level of being and the essential need for a philosophy that integrates into one form social existence and the transcendent power of the transhistorical.

The beginning task in constructing a critical sociology of social existence is, as Zygmunt Bauman phrases it, to "revindicate the social substance of the social world."[12] Existentialists, in refraining from investigating a reality beyond the mental and psychological processes of individuals, retreat into an exploration of the individual's freedom at the periphery of the social world. Furthermore, "they attempt to portray such periphery as a self-sustained world (both cognitively and morally) and, moreover, as the very centre of the life-world from which all other components of this world emanate."[13] Such analysis can never uncover the full meaning of a human existence that is essentially social. In attributing the fundamentals of existence to individual processes—in the face of or in reaction to social reality—an individualistic existentialism fails to allow for the transformation of social existence and the creation of a new world. Emancipation comes out of a historical struggle for social existence, not out of individual and narcissistic revolt.

Let us, then, submit and pursue the following: To be human is to be social; human being is social being. There is no innate self beyond our being in the world collectively. We are—to the extent that we have consciousness—part of the consciousness of the historically created social and cultural world. Human existence is thus social existence. I am the being that is given to me in the social world, which is in union with the order of the universe. We are, together, the consciousness in the universe.

The critical meaning of social existence comes slowly, even in the philosophies and theories that are to be the most social. We struggle to reconstruct a discipline that, however social it may be, tends to emphasize the individual, or the self, at war with "society." A critical sociology is attempting to break the long tradition.

Indeed, there is an extended debate within sociology over the "sociological conception of man."[14] Is "man," for example, the true unit of reality and "society" merely an abstraction representing an accumulation of individual actions? Or is the reality something that may be called "social structure," with little recognition of human intentionality? The dominant view is of an individual-versus-society relationship, with the human being as *Homosociologicus* and a social order made up of such beings.

Whatever the conceptualization, but especially represented in the individual-society conception, there is the failure to consider the quality of the human being. In emphasizing an individualistic voluntarism, supposedly to value the human being, the totality of being human is obscured. To recognize the truly social nature of existence, on the other hand, is to recognize the full potential and reality of being human.

Society, then, is not an abstraction, but the reality within which we human beings become known to each other, which is also to say, to ourselves. As in the central insight of hermeneutical phenomenology, the ontological condition of human existence is a self-understanding that is connected integrally to the understanding shared with others, communicated through the language of the culture, which presupposes a form of life.[15] Social existence is the concrete reality; if there is an abstraction (or a reification), it is the individual. More accurately conceived, holistically, neither society nor the individual is external to the other; both are one. The concrete reality is social existence.

Social existence, therefore, has a meaning in itself. It does not have to be considered as meaningful only when viewed in terms of the operations of individual actions. Social existence is in a continuous process of forming itself, being constituted in a realm where individual human actions and social formations are so integrated that they can no longer be distinguished from one another.

Social existence is always in the process of being transformed, moving in the direction of its own possibility. We all move and have our being in this concrete project. Through our social being—in social existence—we transcend an assumed subjectivity and come to know things as they are. Using the transcendent metaphor, we come to know the word. The totality of the world is uncovered in the historical development of social existence.

The Dialectic of Social Existence

Our social existence, our connectedness in the world, is the reality. Through praxis in the world we transcend the apparent subjectivity of separateness, of individualistic abstraction. The dynamic of social existence is in the relation and tension between origin and goal. Through the striving to overcome the separation from our essential origin and moving to achieve the providential goal inherent in the universe, social existence is continually transformed. It is through social existence and its transformation that our being, which is social, moves in the direction of fulfillment.

Our understanding, as well as our everyday being, is guided by a metaphysic of social existence. Spanning the cultures of the world is a myth about social existence, a myth that is so fundamental to our existence that it is certainly a human archetype. How to characterize the myth within each culture is a problem of symbolization. Drawing from Western cultures, and particularly from some of the symbols found in the Judeo-Christian tradition, we attempt to grasp the essential myth that forms the foundation of contemporary culture, but a myth that has become obscured in the materialistic culture of contemporary (especially capitalist) society. Also the problem is to reconstruct symbols that will be appropriate for the emerging epoch. The reconstructed myth of our origin and goal I shall refer to as the dialectic of social existence.

Two methods of constructing symbols, both forming an essential myth of origin and goal, are evident and can be drawn from to reconstruct a dialectic of social existence. One is represented in the symbolic system constructed in the theology of Paul Tillich, and the other is in the social theory of Karl Marx. Both begin with the questionable character of social existence as manifested in our time. Tillich, involved in the New Hegelian and Marxist intellectual circles between the two world wars and politically active in the socialist movement, placed himself in a prophetic tradition that comes from Marx and, before him, the Old Testament prophets. In his theology, Tillich explored the "profound relationship" between existence and the historical-political situation.[16] The relationship is bound by the character of religion under capitalism, accounting ultimately for the meaninglessness and despair of our time.

Tillich accepted and utilized Marx's critique of bourgeois society, but went beyond its materialist analysis. Marxism is a necessary method of unmasking the hidden levels of secular reality. Its far-reaching religious and historical implications, however, are to be found in its prophetic elements. Socialism, Tillich observes, "acts in the direction of the messianic fulfillment; it is a messianic activity to which everybody is called."[17]

The problem in pursuing only the materialist method is that it denies the urgency of the very human nature that it seeks to unmask and recover. Such a materialist methodology is a false and dogmatic conception of human nature and historical possibility. The urgency of immediate (material) needs actually is often transcended by other, less material needs. We must acknowledge that "even the most pressing needs are colored by their relationship to other needs, by the specific historical situation in which this constellation of factors has come to be."[18] A strictly materialist conception of human nature and historical conditions, in fact, is merely another manifestation of the corruptness of the capitalist order. A restricted materialist analysis is itself a part of the human predicament in contemporary culture.

The methodology for understanding our world as well as our lives within it suffers from the particular capitalist spirit that limits reality to the scientific and technical conquest of time and space. As Tillich describes the condition, "Reality has lost its inner transcendence or, in another metaphor, its transparency for the eternal. The system of finite interrelations which we call the universal has become self-sufficient."[19] Under capitalism, our actual condition is mistakenly regarded as our essential condition. We continue to be the objects of our own history, left to drift without an ultimate end. This truly is the contemporary human predicament.

The basic question asked in both Marxism and prophetic theology is the relation between *existence* and *essence*— between our essential nature and our existential situation. In both the theology of Tillich and the social theory of Marx there are three fundamental concepts that characterize the problem of existence and essence: essential goodness, existential estrangement, and the possibility of something else through which the separation is overcome. In secular Marxian form, the separation of existence and essence, of the "is" and

the "ought," is the tragic interpretation of social life. Alienation is the product of a special historical situation, and can be
overcome only through human action. In the secular form,
however, various kinds of human suffering continue to hold
true even after the transformation of capitalism. What Tillich
calls for in his theology is an image of finite existence that is
tied to a concern about the infinite. Essence, in other words,
is not merely a characterization of a possible finite existence,
but also an absolute beyond the possibility of any specific
finite reality. Going further than an existential philosophy, to
what may be called a theological *essentialism*, Tillich holds
out the possibility of knowing (by grace of faith) the ultimate questions and meaning of life.[20] We may know, or at
least attend to, an objective essence beyond finite existence
when we allow ourselves to consider infinite being in the
universe.

Yet it is the prophetic voice in Marx that has drawn us to
the questions of theology. There is a rediscovery of the
eschatological dimension in both Marxism and theology, a
new consideration of the transformation of the world and an
opening of the future.[21] Marxism and theology confront
each other in ways that allow us to understand our condition
and to consider our essential social and transhistorical existence.

The prophetic theory formulated by Marx, distinguishing
between existence and essence, is confined to the secular
world. Prophetic theology, on the other hand, attempts to
relate existence and essence in the secular world to state-
ments and symbols about the sacred. Marxism has its own
metaphysic—the prophetic—but it is confined to matters of
the material world.[22] What is necessary, I am suggesting, is a
reconstruction of the dialectic of social existence, the integration of the sacred and the secular into a single symbolic
system. The result would be a holistic image of social exis-

tence and its transformation, an image that would unite the historical and the transhistorical, the finite and the infinite.

One way to attempt the union of the sacred and the secular is by means of correlation. While Marx excluded the transhistorical from the historical, Tillich considered both by constructing a system of parallel symbols. This was accomplished by relating the crucial areas of human existence to the transcendent symbols of Christianity. The existing Christian beliefs and symbols were brought to bear on the contemporary problems of existence. In his own description of the method, Tillich states that "in using the method of correlation, systematic theology proceeds in the following way: it makes an analysis of the human situation out of which the existential questions arise, and it demonstrates that the symbols used in the Christian message are the answers to these questions."[23] The system then falls into five parts, each with a discussion of an aspect of human existence, on the one hand, and an interpretation through Christian symbols on the other. The five parts, with their correlations, are reason and revelation, being and God, existence and the Christ, life and the Spirit, history and the kingdom of God.[24]

The method that I am proposing—on the dialectic of social existence—differs from the correlation method by integrating the secular and the sacred into single symbols. It also differs from the substance of Tillich's system by moving beyond the individualistic existentialism implied in his religious symbols and categories of human existence. Thus, the dialectic of social existence (1) *integrates* the sacred and the secular into a series of composite symbols and (2) denotes the realm of *social* existence. The aim is to reconstruct the critical meaning of social existence.

We are working within the three fundamental themes of human culture. The three themes form the basis for the myths that pervade all cultures, representing the universals of

social existence. In the dialectic, and in the search for the
meaning of social existence, these themes are, with their
alternative designations:

Social Order	Social Disorder	Social Transformation
Absolute reality	Separation	Integration
Essence	Alienation	Revolution
Creation	Sinfulness	Redemption

Combined and considered simultaneously the three dimensions constitute social existence. In dialectical relation and
tension, they are the source of history and represent the
transhistorical in the transformation of human history. For
purposes of elaboration, each dimension of social existence
can be considered separately.

The meaning of human existence begins with the drama of
the creation. All other experiences become apprehensible in
relation to the fundamental reality that was there at the
beginning. Represented variously as our human origin, the
state of innocence, our essential nature before the separation
of spirit and matter, and actual or absolute reality, a characterization of our beginning contributes to all cultural myths
of social existence. For Marx a basic and universal human
nature, a "species-being," was present in the creation of the
human being; and as species-being we continually recreate
our lives.[25] The beginning, in Christian theology, means
being as goodness: "God saw everything that he created, and
behold, it was good."[26] All subsequent history and religious
experience is in reference to the original state of existence.
Social order is contained in our origin in nature and the
universe.

Following upon the drama of the creation is the drama of
the "fall." As soon as the world is created with human

beings, there takes place the tragedy of the loss of innocence, the eating of the forbidden fruit, the separation of the human being from God.[27] With knowledge and human conscious- ness we become separated from our origin. In the secular phrasing of Marxism, the production of life itself becomes alienated, especially under the capitalist mode of produc- tion.[28] Social order has fallen to the disordered condition in the historical development of capitalism. True humanity can be achieved only in a protest against this estrangement, a humanity revitalized with the religious as well as the mate- rial.[29] *Social disorder* is necessarily and ultimately to be overcome.

The disorder that is a consequence of the alienation and separation between the original state and the present condi- tion is traditionally called, in theological and religious terms, "sin." Sin is separation, a separation of our contemporary existence from our essential nature, a separation between finite possibility and the infinite ground of our being. We are bound to that ground even in separation, Tillich writes, referring to Kierkegaard's observations:

> We always remain in the power of that from which we are estranged. The fact brings us to the ultimate depth of sin: separated and yet bound, estranged and yet belonging, destroyed and yet preserved, the state which is called despair. Despair means that there is no escape. Despair is "the sickness unto death."[30]

In traditional terms, "hell" is the condition of ultimate separation and the place where we are fated to because of our separation. Sin is a loss of faith in God, an alienation from the essential ground of our being.

Only redemption and salvation can lead to the original state and heal the separation after the fall.[31] Only redemption and salvation can bring light back into the world, uniting existence with essential nature. Although redemption in the theological sense is outside history, in the realm of the transhistorical, there is nevertheless a secular redemption that eliminates the alienation in our present historical predicament. From the analysis of alienation in contemporary society emerges the possibility of a revolution that will allow human beings to achieve their potential and society to become ordered once again. [32] Because the conditions under which everyday life takes place in present society are contradictory and defeating, divorcing us from our essential function, transformation of the world becomes necessary. The Marxist critique of the secular political economy incorporates the call as well as the prescription for redemption, a redemption in the historical condition. *Social transformation* moves in the direction of fulfillment.

Social existence is the dialectic of social order, social disorder, and social transformation. Within the dialectic of social existence, human beings become alienated and seek to overcome that alienation; social arrangements become contradictory and separated from their essential order. Social disorder, in turn, is constantly in a dialectic to recover its inherent order.

Whenever there is the attempt on the part of human intelligence to understand the dialectic of social existence, there tends to be a separation between a historical (secular) understanding and a transhistorical (sacred) understanding. A religious terminology normally uses a traditional metaphysic, and a secular terminology usually confines understanding to the finite historical. In a holistic understanding, however, we seek to unite the sacred and the secular, the historical and the ultimate. The dialectic of social existence is made whole in an understanding that places the historical condition in relation to the metaphysic of universal meaning. The critical meaning of social existence is in a dialectic of the essential dimensions of social existence with the matters of ultimate consequence. Social existence is in union and tension with universal purpose.

Critical Reflection

We remain within the grasp of the prophetic; all moves in the direction of a universal fulfillment. There is a meaning in the universe, and social existence is the breaking of universal meaning into the historical, the meaning of the universe becoming known in the concrete world of everyday life. The faith, whether in our science or in our daily lives, is represented in the metaphysical symbol of providence. All things work together ultimately for the good, as Tillich notes:

> Faith in divine Providence is the faith that nothing can prevent us from fulfilling the ultimate meaning of our existence. Providence does not mean a divine planning by which everything is predetermined, as in an efficient machine. Rather, Providence means that there is a creative and saving possibility implied in every situation, which cannot be destroyed by any event. Providence means that the daemonic and destructive forces within ourselves and our world can never have an unbreakable grasp upon us, and that the bond which connects us with the fulfilling love can never be disrupted.[33]

Our struggle is for the realization of a social existence that fulfills the promise and the hope.

The task of a sustained critical reflection in the world is the struggle for social existence. The purpose is to make known the particular dialectic of social existence within the concrete historical and social situation. Critical reflection offers the possibility of understanding such that we as social beings come to know ourselves and our situation.[34] In a holistic image, combining secular and sacred goals, we come to know the world critically and understand its meaning in the larger universe.

Moreover, in an understanding that is concrete while it is also metaphysically grounded, we engage in the reconstruction of our social existence in accordance with a meaning that is both temporal and universal. Critical reflection—a form that is prophetically critical, Marxian in theory and practice, and theologically philosophical—is a practice that is part of the reconstruction of social existence and is a force in the reconstruction.

The emancipatory possibility of critical reflection is in coming to know the concrete historical conditions that are preventing the realization of human possibility.[35] But the possibility is not confined only to the realization of individual possibilities and to secular pursuits; emancipation is also in the realization of a true social existence and in a social existence that is grounded in universal meaning. The demystification that is possible in a prophetically related social theory involves an uncovering of the conditions that thwart a social existence that is both concretely and sacredly significant. Such a critical theory makes known to us the way in which the ultimate meaning of social existence is being prevented from breaking into the contemporary historical situation. Knowing the constraints being placed on the present condition, in an understanding that is both concrete and metaphysical, we can move from the deconstruction provided by our understanding to the reconstruction. The reconstruction is in our mental faculties, in our spiritual being, and in the creation of the everyday actions and social structures of existence.

That social existence is being constrained from its possibility by distorted communication is part of the message of critical sociology.[36] Again, for us, the hermeneutical character of existence is emphasized. How we conceive of the world and how we convey to each other through speech the meaning of our existence is a problem of hermeneutics. The world is to be interpreted, and how we interpret it (in academic pursuits or in everyday life) is of consequence to the kind of world we create and the way we understand the meaning of that world. Critical reflection is a part of the process of interpretation and creation; it is not separate from everyday reality, as assumed in a positivistic, noncritical social science. Critical reflection speaks in a way that is appropriate for the everyday reconstruction of the world.

It is my argument that the speech of critical reflection must appeal to the human needs that are both material and spiritual, concrete-historical and transcendent. The hermeneutic of critical reflection is metaphysically grounded as well as attendant to the concrete world—and it applies to the concrete world because it is of metaphysical significance. This is to say, also, a critical social science is more than "the emancipation of reason" for the purpose of material emancipation.[37] It certainly is an emancipation of reason, through language and knowledge, for the betterment of material conditions, but it is also the emancipation of the spiritual and sacred character of existence. Emancipation—the realization of social existence—is a project of the reconciliation of both spirit and matter.

Our language for interpretation and understanding—for the construction of meaning—certainly comes out of the structure of existence, out of the form of life.[38] Our understanding is constructed out of symbols that have been created and structured in material reality. But, contrary to a strictly materialist and reductionist structuralism, the symbols are a breaking out of the material and into the universal. Our human constructions are created out of a structure that is both materially and metaphysically significant. Social existence is an expression of material life *and* meaning in the universe. An understanding of our existence, coming from social existence, is certainly materially based, but is founded on that which transcends the material and gives the material its meaning. Meaning, therefore, is ultimately within social existence because it is the universe entering into existence. Without social existence there could be no meaning, no possibility of the meaning becoming known.

Social existence, in a critical social theory, is conceived as part of the process of the coming into being of social existence—as the struggle for social existence. The meaning of social existence, similarly, is a part of the process of the coming into being of meaning.[39] Nothing in the universe is to be singularly and absolutely grasped without the medium of understanding in social context. What we bring into existence through our understanding is not the original being and meaning, but the interpretation of the meaning of the living present with all of its ultimate significance. A search for the absolute—out of contemporary historical context—is the false recovery of a dead and inappropriate meaning. Critical reflection is a meditation on the present social and historical condition and its meaning in the universal scheme of things. Through reconstructed consciousness and existence, truth is manifested in our time.

Our critical and prophetic understanding is in the recognition of the social disorder of contemporary social existence. That we are held within the grasp of what could be—of what is essential social order—is the providential character of critical reflection. The prophetic hope and demand is to reconstruct our social existence, bringing contemporary existence into essence, disorder into order through social transformation. With an apprehension of the universal in history, we reconstruct our social existence.

To recognize that understanding about social existence cannot be reached entirely within social existence is the recognition and faith of a critical reflection. To attempt to understand ourselves (our social existence) out of ourselves is a fallacy. Gadamer observes that "it is an age-old motif of faith, which already pervades Augustine's reflection on his life, that all of man's efforts to understand himself out of himself, and in terms of the world over which he presides as his own, ultimately founder."[40] Our understanding—our existence, in other words—is related to the metaphysical character of our existence. Critical sociology is a shattering of the "self-sufficiency" of a solely material analysis. Understanding necessarily comes out of that which is revealed in the material but is manifested outside it. There can be no critical reflection without a recognition of the metaphysical grounding of social existence.

When we apprehend the order of the universe and our place within it as realized in the social order of existence, and when we understand the meaning of social existence in our search and struggle for social existence, we begin to find a home in the world. When we have been opened to a hearing of the word, we are at a place in the universe where our existence has meaning. We seek life in the transformation that is material and spiritual, in the struggle for social existence.

NOTES

1. George Rupp, *Beyond Existentialism and Zen: Religion in a Pluralistic World* (New York: Oxford University Press, 1979), p. 11.

2. See David Tracy, "Metaphor and Religion: The Test Case of Christian Texts," *Critical Inquiry*, 5 (Autumn 1978), pp. 93-95.

3. Ernest Becker, *The Denial of Death* (New York: Free Press, 1973), p. 51.

4. *Ibid., p. 50.*

5. *Ibid.*, p. 153.

6. John Macquarrie, *Existentialism* (New York: Penguin Books, 1972), pp. 16-17.

7. See *ibid.*, pp. 279-281.

8. Robert Coles, *Walker Percy: An American Search* (Boston: Little, Brown, 1978), p. 164.

9. Gabriel Marcel, *The Mystery of Being* (London: Harvill Press, 1951), p. 33.

10. See the commentaries in Kenneth T. Gallagher, *The Philosophy of Gabriel Marcel* (New York: Fordham University Press, 1962); John B. O'Malley, *The Fellowship of Being: An Essay on the Concept of Person in the Philosophy of Gabriel Marcel* (The Hague, Netherlands: Martinus Nijhoff, 1966).

11. Gabriel Marcel, *The Philosophy of Existentialism* (New York: Citadel Press, 1961), p. 88.

12. Zygmunt Bauman, *Towards a Critical Sociology: An Essay on Commonsense and Emancipation* (London: Routledge & Kegan Paul, 1976), p. 84.

13. *Ibid.*

14. See Barry Smart, *Sociology, Phenomenology and Marxian Analysis: A Critical Discussion of the Theory and Practice of a Science of Society* (London: Routledge & Kegan Paul, 1976), pp. 137-146.

15. Anthony Giddens, *New Rules of Sociological Method: A Positive Critique of Interpretative Sociologies* (New York: Basic Books, 1976), p. 19.

16. See James L. Adams, "Introduction," in Paul Tillich, *Political Expectation* (New York: Harper & Row, 1971), pp. ix-x.

17. Paul Tillich, *Theology of Culture*, ed. Robert C. Kimball (New York: Oxford University Press, 1959), p. 198.

18. Paul Tillich, *The Socialist Decision*, trans. Franklin Sherman (New York: Harper & Row, 1977), p. 114.

19. Tillich, *Theology of Culture*, pp. 43-44.

20. *Ibid.*, pp. 76-111.

21. See, for example, José Miguez Bonino, *Doing Theology in a Revolutionary Situation* (Philadelphia: Fortress Press, 1975); Gustavo Gutiérrez, *A Theology of Liberation: History, Politics and Salvation*, trans. and ed. Sister Caridad Inda and John Eagleson (Maryknoll, NY: Orbis, 1973); José Miranda, *Marx and the Bible: A Critique of the Philosophy of Oppression*, trans. John Eagleson (Maryknoll, NY: Orbis, 1974).

22. See Arend Theodoor van Leeuwen, *Critique of Heaven* (New York: Scribner, 1972).

23. Paul Tillich, *Systematic Theology*, Vol. 1 (Chicago: University of Chicago Press, 1951), p. 62.

24. The correlation method, with special reference to the symbol of God, is discussed in William L. Rowe, *Religious Symbols and God: A Philosophical Study of Tillich's Theology* (Chicago: University of Chicago Press, 1968).

25. See James M. Glass, "Marx, Kafka, and Jung: The Appearance of Species-Being," *Politics and Society*, 2 (Winter 1972), pp. 255-271.

26. Tillich, *Theology of Culture*, pp. 118-119.

27. On the myth of the creation and the fall, see Paul Ricoeur, *The Symbolism of Evil*, trans. Emerson Buchanan (Boston: Beacon Press, 1967), pp. 172-174.

28. Karl Marx, *The Grundrisse*, ed. David McLellan (New York: Harper & Row, 1971), pp. 132-143.

29. Tillich, *Political Expectation*, pp. 90-91.

30. Paul Tillich, *The Shaking of the Foundations* (New York: Scribner, 1955), p. 160.

31. See the discussion of Jonathan Edwards's theology of redemption in Sydney E. Ahlstrom, *A Religious History of the American People* (New Haven: Yale University Press, 1972), pp. 305-313.

32. See Stanley Aronowitz, "Culture and Politics," *Politics and Society*, 6, 3 (1976), pp. 347-376.

33. Tillich, *Shaking*, pp. 106-107.

34. Smart, *Sociology, Phenomenology, and Marxian Analysis*, p. 184.

35. Bauman, *Towards a Critical Sociology*, pp. 1-4.

36. See Jürgen Habermas, *Theory and Practice*, trans. John Viertel (Boston: Beacon Press, 1973); Zygmunt Bauman, *Hermeneutics and Social Science* (New York: Columbia University Press, 1978).

37. Bauman, *Towards a Critical Sociology*, p. 112.

38. See Rosalind Coward and John Ellis, *Language and Materialism: Developments in Semiology and the Theory of the Subject* (London: Routledge & Kegan Paul, 1977).

39. For a discussion of this sense of the hermeneutic, see Hans-Georg Gadamer, *Truth and Method* (New York: Seabury Press, 1975), pp. 146-150.

40. Hans-Georg Gadamer, *Philosophical Hermeneutics*, trans. and ed. David E. Linge (Berkeley: University of California Press, 1976), p. 206; John O'Neill, *Making Sense Together: An Introduction to Wild Sociology* (New York: Harper & Row, 1974).

5

Struggle for
Social Existence

Meaning is both found and created in the struggle for social existence. The movement is toward a social existence that makes possible the fulfillment of the prophetic goal, where existence and essence come together. In the struggle for social existence, the conditions—social, economic, political, and religious—are created for the realization of a meaning charged with the depth of reality, a world in which historical existence is in relation to ultimate purpose. According to the symbols of our tradition, "the temporal is elevated into the eternal and the eternal becomes effective in the realm of time."[1]

Social existence and our struggle for it are simultaneously (to use the traditional metaphysic) holy and profane. Where the secular is, there also is the sacred. In spite of the contemporary effort to separate the two, the metaphysic of existence presupposes their union into a single realm. Neither the secular nor the sacred is or can ever be completely autonomous. The secular is the reality of everyday life in the presence of the sacred. It is merely the extent to which the historical has become separated from the transcendent—and the extent to which the metaphysical is excluded from everyday life and the larger social reality—that enables us to talk about the secular and the sacred as distinct from each other.

The primary definition of what it is to be human and to be in social existence comes from the metaphysic of our existence, realized to whatever degree in our historical existence. That to a large extent the secular has become separated from the sacred is the condition of contemporary social existence. The struggle for social existence is for the transformation of the conditions that will allow the eternal to break into the finite, making social existence possible.

Moral Existence

Life in contemporary times, especially under capitalism, has come largely to be conditionally determined. The everyday morality of social life has become separated from the unconditional source. Human social existence tends to be dictated by historically specific goals and demands, tied to the particular interests of capitalism. The social and moral problems of today are to a large degree a result of the historical nexus of capitalist development and the relative exclusion of the sacred—a result of the exclusion of the unconditional nature of human social existence from everyday life.

There also has been a steady capitulation of religion to capitalism. A religion that is gradually removed from the unconditional questions and answers of our lives and the universe, tied instead primarily to the thoughts conditioned by the present age, becomes a decadent force in modern life. Religious life becomes as alienated as the political, social, and economic life of the society.

Religious life is transformed into that which fits into the alienated culture of capitalism. Even in much of religious revival, as Erich Fromm has noted, "the belief in God has been transformed into a psychological device to make one better fitted for the competitive struggle."[2] Just as we and our labor become commodities under capitalism, religion tends to be a commodity in the everyday marketplace of life.

The struggle to be whole again—the struggle to reconcile our existence with our essential nature—therefore involves a transformation that is both material and transcendent.

A religion that once helped to shape culture has come to be a tool of the culture of advanced capitalism. Religion has largely become bound within capitalist culture. As James Luther Adams writes, much of contemporary religion

> has lost its relatedness to an ultimate ground and aim, and thus it has lost much of its original prophetic power. Its God has become domesticated; it is a bourgeois god. In its major effect its ethics are largely indistinguishable from the "ethics" of the bourgeois principle.[3]

As a consequence, contemporary religion mainly aggravates the contradictions of capitalist society. Through its emphasis on economic and spiritual individualism and its class-bound moralism, religion (as embodied especially in Protestant Christianity) has become a cause as well as a symptom of the crisis of contemporary capitalist society. If religion is to play a prophetic and creative role in its own transformation and in the transformation of capitalist culture, it must effect a profound break with the bourgeois principle.

The moral transformation is to be grounded in the unconditioned for all that exists conditionally. Through faith in the unconditional ground of our being, we and the world are transformed. Being religious is being unconditionally concerned, although religion is realized conditionally in the concrete social existence. The prophetic principle is unconditionally grounded, but it is humanly realized in the construction of social existence.

The idea that moral principles are categorical or unconditional in form goes beyond the *moralism* that characterizes any moral consideration in secular society. Moralism is the contemporary attitude, a negative attitude toward life that is a distortion of the moral imperative.[4] Moralism is an oppressive demand that is without grounding in anything beyond itself, other than perhaps an archaic culture. *Morality*, on the other hand, is conscious of its historical roots and is grounded in a transcendent principle that gives unconditional meaning to the moral act. Without this grounding, the moral act is completely secular and lacking in ultimate concern.

The prophetic message, as Tillich notes, is that a new reality has appeared with the coming of Christ, "a power of being in which we can participate, and out of which true thought and action can follow, however fragmentarily."[5] It is in such a transcendent religious spirit that we are grounded in what is ultimate and unconditioned in being and meaning. The moral imperative, in this grounding, is "the demand to become actually what one is essentially and therefore potentially," the true being becoming the actual being within the worldly community.[6] The moral imperative is religious in its unconditional character. In following the moral imperative, we are grounded in an ultimate concern, by that which is seriously taken unconditionally. Morality, beyond secular ethics and any concrete religion, is the prophetic entering into social existence.

In the conceptualization of the struggle for social existence that I am presenting, then, all action takes place within some kind of moral framework. Human action is necessarily moral action. Human behavior is carried out with justification, with moral grounding. Whether in our social-scientific understanding of action or in the explanation of action by the actors themselves, human action is directed and understood in terms of its moral context.[7] Our descriptions of the world are couched in moral terms, no matter how "objective" we pretend to be. The social sciences, and all other human endeavors, are "moral sciences."[8] When we inquire into human action, social existence, and the meaning of it all, we are operating firmly within a moral existence. The important question is, however, what is the particular grounding of our morality?

The question is not usually raised nowadays, either in social science or in other everyday life, because (in part at least) the contemporary social conditions that would make such discourse fully possible do not exist. Similarly, a consideration of morality is obscured by an emphasis on other conceptions of morality. Thus, the literary critic Terry Eagleton writes, "if Marxism has had little to say directly about the 'moral,' one reason for this obliquity is that one does not engage in moral debate with those for whom morality can only mean moralism."[9] We need, in other words, to transcend the narrow conception of morality (as moralism) that grounds contemporary social existence. And this is accomplished not by will itself, but by the struggle for a new social existence.

We return to the matter of attending to the unconditional grounding of the moral imperative. That grounding in the Western world traditionally has been in the Judeo-Christian tradition. There are certainly other sources for giving foundation to the morality of social existence. There may be symbols that are more appropriate for the world we are creating. But the reconstruction of our symbols most certainly begins within the inherited cultural tradition. While morality is contained within finite possibilities, it is assumed to be grounded in and pointing to something beyond itself. That morality has lost its depth of meaning—its unconditionality— in modern times is the critical beginning of a reconstruction. The reconstruction of moral existence, including its grounding in a metaphysic, is part of the struggle for social existence. Without the depth of grounding there can be no reconstruction of social existence. The meaning of social existence is in the grounding of the morality of that existence.

From the inherited tradition, morality without a religious grounding is one that does not affirm our essential prophetic being. An "autonomous morality" is incapable of ascertaining our essential nature because of its separation from essential being, because of our fallen state.[10] Such a morality is mistaken, false, and ill-conceived; it is a shallow and conditional morality. Thus there is the need today in the reconciliation that is both existential and transcendent (worldly revolutionary and sacredly religious) for a theonomous morality, a morality grounded in the religious spirit. No matter how much the contents of the morality—of a socialist morality—are conditioned by the current situation, the general moral imperative in our reconstruction is unconditionally grounded. The conditioned character of concrete historical morality does not contradict the unconditional validity of the moral imperative itself.[11] To establish the reunion of our essential nature with our actual nature is the purpose of the struggle for social existence.

Social and Spiritual Existence

The modern world has become "secularized" to the extent that the sacred is relegated to a separate compartment of social existence, if the sacred is recognized at all. Secularity has become the spiritual equivalent of advanced capitalism. We are, however, in a critical and prophetic sociology, engaged in a reflection and a practice that goes beyond this secularity, toward the emergence of a postsecular, metaphysically informed society. We are moving toward an age where our recourse is not limited to the ability of the supposedly autonomous individual to deal with matters of existence in a totally secular world. In going beyond the secular age, the sacred and the secular become one, and human social existence is in the world and at the same time is informed by ultimate concerns of universal nature.

Currently, discussions of the role and future of religion in modern society, especially those by sociologists, tend to assume the continuation of a capitalist, secular society. Although there are considerable differences in the arguments, focusing mainly on the extent to which religion has meaning in contemporary society, the underlying assumption tends to be that American society (as well as the Western world) will remain basically the same, with perhaps further secularization. The analyses of contemporary religion center on such issues as the privatization of religion (Thomas Luckmann), a societal as well as civil religion (J. Paul Williams), a continuing pattern of traditional religion (Andrew M. Greeley), the emergence of alternative religions (Charles Y. Glock and Robert N. Bellah), and the continuing human need for a transcendental religion (Peter L. Berger).[12] The prognosis in these accounts is that, while religion is becoming more flexible in form and content, it will continue to evolve and to be a force in society and to have an effect on individual life. Yet, these accounts and their forecasts fail to consider the development of religion beyond secularized capitalism. The conventional question is whether a religion may function in a secularized capitalist society. The search is for a meaningful religion in the existing capitalist society. However, it is in the evolving socialist order, and in the struggle for a socialist society, that the creation of the religion for the future is taking place.

To argue for a recovery of the sacred and the metaphysical, as I have been doing throughout, is not to suggest that religion must stand outside culture. On the contrary, I am contending that the transcendental is known only—and can only operate—in the everyday world of human and social life. Even in the most secular of cultures, there is the sacred that can shape and transform our lives, to say nothing about guiding us in our most mundane affairs. Our metaphysic is active in contemporary culture, in a secular culture that is coming to recognize the universal in the struggle for a socialist society.

Matters of metaphysical import are coming to be a part of the world, rather than standing outside it. The transcendent has meaning only in and through social existence, in turn giving meaning to social existence. Struggling for social existence is not, by definition, secular; it is being in the world with a relation to and a concern for the transcendent, the universal, the metaphysical. In the ultimate union of daily life and social existence, the conventional secular-sacred dichotomy is surpassed. Our struggle in the world is made real and meaningful by its relation to what the world can become.

A social existence that is also a spiritual existence—as it certainly must be in order to be whole—liberates the human being from a self-seeking life to an involvement in and a commitment to the struggle for social existence. In bringing the secular and the sacred together, the everyday life with ultimate concern, the narcissistic and self-limiting character of a completely secular life is overcome.[13] In attending to that which gives transcendent meaning to our existence, the measure of all things is more than ourselves; meaning is to be found in a world shared with others and defined by the ultimate meaning of social existence. We find ourselves only when we are placed in (when we are "lost" in) the larger social world, one that is filled with ultimate and universal meaning. And the commitment to the struggle for social existence is, to use a principal metaphor from the Judeo-Christian tradition, love, the revelation of the true meaning of the universe.[14]

That metaphysical considerations, especially as found in Christianity, tend to promote a conservative force in social existence is a common claim in arguments that seek to advance the purely secular cause. Marx's observation that the social effects of religion can limit social action is often cited to discredit not only the practice of religion but theological claims about the sacred as well. Some religions, or religions at some times, do turn attention away from social struggles, concentrating instead on individual salvation. The major religions follow a two-world theory of existence, where the reality that is not seen (particularly the nontemporal) is regarded as more important than the everyday life of social existence.

But contrary to the nontemporal emphasis, existence is, in fact, given meaning by the sacred demand. An observer of the social effects of religion notes:

> The religious call to renunciation has meant renouncing one's profits from the social establishment as often as it has meant a renunciation of a concern for temporal justice. Although some religions in some places may have induced people to neglect the hard work of justice, there are enough counter examples to make the criticism inapplicable to the essential religious needs of life.[15]

The Marxist criticism of religion is directed not against the importance of a religious metaphysic, but against concrete examples of religion practiced in a nonprohetic way.

The emphasis on spiritual existence has prompted and increased the struggle for social existence as much or more than it has suggested that people wait for a better life hereafter. The spiritual in the temporal life, in fact, gives foundation to the movement for a better social existence. Hence:

> The Marxist criticism of religion as a source of social conservatism has only partial historical truth; sometimes

religion has been that, and sometimes not. There is
nothing essential to religion as a social response to
absolute existence which requires it. On the contrary,
religion tends to have social bite just because it recognizes that the divine perspective calls all human perspec-
tives to account.[16]

The religious, or some form of the metaphysical, continues to
give meaning (and ultimate meaning) to the everyday struggles for social existence.

The search for a religiously based social existence has been
shaped in recent years by an increasing concern about the
future of contemporary cultures. The impetus of this concern
is brought about by several world historical events, including
the increasing development of science and technology, the
emergence of the Third World of newly decolonized nations,
the development of socialism in many nations, and the
internal political developments within both communist and
capitalist nations.[17] In relation to these concrete developments there has emerged a "Marxist-Christian dialogue" that
is addressed not only to the future of the world but also to
the necessity of forming an alliance between Marxism and
religion in assuring a future.

Marxism is a dynamic philosophy and practice that is
constantly being shaped and reformulated in the course of
human struggle. The defense of atheism in Marxism is currently being revised among Marxists. While Herbert Aptheker
states that "according to the materialist view of the problem
of causation, consciousness does not precede reality," and
that "this position is fundamental to Marxism and absolutely
basic to its program of determining what is wrong in society
and how to correct it," more recent Marxist formulations
consider the dialectic that takes place between the material
substructure and the nonmaterial superstructure.[18] The more
progressive conception of the relationship is incorporated in a

conception proposed sometime ago by Tillich: "The economic sphere is itself a complex sphere, to which all other spheres essentially contribute, so that they cannot be derived from it, although they never can be separated from it."[19] Religion certainly cannot be rejected out of a contention that as part of the superstructure it is unimportant; religion is part of the consciousness that shapes the objective conditions of history.

Marxist humanism, however, has traditionally excluded the religiously transcendent from its analysis and practice. Although Marxism does not necessarily begin from a theoretical atheism, its secular position is a logical consequence of a humanism that exalts "man" to supreme importance and denies the existence of any meaning that might transcend the human being. At the present moment in the dialectic, Marxists are learning about transcendence and theologians are learning about revolutionary practice. Instead of the debate being limited to questions about the finite versus the infinite, the dialectic of Marxism and religion can be fulfilled in the critical and prophetic theology that emerges in relation to concrete practice.[20] Complete insistence on a secular humanism is not in itself an innate presupposition of Marxism; and avoidance of revolutionary involvement in the secular world certainly is not a necessary or a historical characteristic of religion.[21] The purpose of religion is to change the world in anticipation of the kingdom of true social existence.

The dialectic in the Marxist-Christian debate continues as long as Marxist humanism excludes the transcendent. The dialectic ceases and an integration of Marxism and theology takes place when the secular eschatology of Marxism becomes a sacred eschatology as well. The integration is entirely plausible and likely insofar as Marxism has its eschatological roots in the Judeo-Christian tradition. As Adams has observed, "Marx's humanism—his intention to promote the full realization of the potentialities of human-

ity—cannot be viewed as something completely unique that
bears no positive relation to the previous Judeo-Christian
humanism."[22] The materialism of Marxism, rather than
being the opposite of Christianity, incorporates the central
doctrine that is committed to the significance of the historical process.

The faith of a theological Marxism is grounded both in
history and in the grace of its transcendence. The ideal of
human fulfillment, in the conflict between justice and injus-
tice, is the universal value shared by Marxism and prophetic
religion. Marxism and religion are expressions of a universal
truth that points toward a redemption to which we all aspire.
As Shepherd Bliss, a participant in the theology of liberation,
writes, "The problem is not whether we are Christians or
Marxists, but whether—as Christians, Marxists, or whatever—
our lives point beyond themselves and are united with others
struggling for justice." [23] The radical immanence of Marxism
and the transcendent power of prophetic theology are integrated and realized in and through our struggle for a socialist
existence.

Socialist Existence

The struggle for social existence is simultaneously historical and metaphysical, one always informing the other. The
universal expressions that are socialist and religious continue
to be manifested in human history as they always have been.
The communal-religious movements and the Christian socialism of the present century are concrete manifestations of
that universal truth that joins immanent social life with
transcendent symbolism. In our own age, the secular humanism of Marxism and religious humanism combined in religious
socialism.

In the broadest of terms, religion and socialism are brought together by the basic dynamic of the sacred and the secular, by the integration of religion and culture. It is religion, as ultimate concern, that gives meaning to the substance of culture; and culture is the totality of forms in which the basic concern of religion expresses itself.[24] Every religious act is culturally formed, and the content of every cultural form is an expression of religion in its deepest sense. Religion is known through our culture as it historically develops. Religious socialism thus represents in our own time the essential unity of religion and culture. Universal meaning is realized through and shapes our struggle for a socialist culture in this world. It is in the socialist struggle of this world at this time that we recognize the transcendent.

As Tillich considered the possibilities of religious socialism, he probed the elemental roots of both religion and socialism, hoping for the transformation of both. His concern with religion and socialism was with much more than how the workers could be won back to the church.[25] Nor was he attempting to lure the workers away from socialist parties, although others might use a Christian socialism for just such purpose. Rather, Tillich was seeking a religious dimension for socialism. By uncovering the roots of socialism in its secular eschatology and its propheticism in a "self-sufficient world," he made socialists aware of the faith already present in the socialist vision, and sought to transform the vision into the truly religious realm as well. An interpreter of this aspect of Tillich's project, John R. Strumme, observes that Tillich was bringing into awareness the common faith expressed in the prophetic-eschatological symbol of the kingdom of God:

> His theological interpretation turns on this symbol. One might even say that the theological thrust of his religious socialism was to discover the concrete social and

political meaning of the prayer, "Thy kingdom come."
The kingdom comes in history, yet remains transcendent; the kingdom is "at hand," but it cannot be pos-
sessed. Its character is paradoxical: the transcendent is
not in an undialectical opposition to history, but shows
its genuine transcendence by breaking into history, shattering and changing it.[26]

The union of the future-oriented symbol of socialist expectation with the sacred propheticism of the Judeo-Christian
heritage is accomplished in a religious socialism.

With its roots in the universal demand, socialism has historically had the power to move the proletariat—and the
proletariat particularly. It has made the proletariat self-
conscious of its destiny. "For in the universal tendency of
socialism," writes Tillich, "is expressed the will of the proletariat to move beyond itself—not in the sense of an upward
mobility into the bourgeois class, but in the sense of a new
form of human being and of society as a whole."[27] Through
the desire for and an expectation of the classless society, the
proletariat has placed itself in historical contexts that surpass
its particular form of being. Neither standing as a general
demand over against history nor representing a special empirical case, socialism is a particular principle that at the same
time expresses human being in general—an expectation of the
new. This is its universality, reaching back to the origins of
life. It is based on the inseparable connection between the
universal socialist principle and the concrete struggles of
those who labor in society.

A socialist existence as thus conceived is the image upon
which the critique of existing society rests and the image of
the future possibility of our social existence. Bauman writes:

Socialism shares with all other utopias the unpleasant
quality of retaining its fertility only in so far as it resides

in the realm of the possible. The moment it is pro-
claimed as accomplished, as empirical reality, it loses its
creative power; far from inflaming human imagination,
it puts on the agenda in turn an acute demand for a new
horizon, distant enough to transcend and relativize its
own limitations.[28]

Socialism is an ideal always to be realized.

As a social existence, socialism is the system that "best
allows the application of rationality to the interests of the
community taken as a whole."[29] On the economic level,
socialism is the transition from a market economy to a
planned economy that is responsive to human needs. It
involves a planning of the economy for the benefit of all in
the society, rather than for the profit of the capitalist class. It
allows for the participation of the greatest number in the
decisions within the society.

But socialism in practice is always in danger of being
reduced to the original objective of the capitalist society
from which it emerges. Ricoeur observes:

Bourgeois society conceived capitalism itself as the
means to achieve, through competition, the spirit of
enterprise, risks and gambles, the fundamental objec-
tives of an utilitarian ethics. Socialism could turn out
only to be, by means of superior rationality and better
technology, the resumption of the same hedonistic
ethics; socialism would then only be a more advanced
and more rational industrialism pursuing the same
dream of the Promethean conquest of well-being and of
nature. It would only have pursued in a more rational
way mastery of the world by means of a society geared
to total satisfaction.[30]

A developing socialist society cannot be devoid of ethical and
spiritual concerns; otherwise the ideal will never be realized.

A socialist existence has to combine the rational planning of the material realm with ultimate concerns. Socialism is a material *and* spiritual existence. It is more than the conquering of the economy and the production of abundance; it is also the fulfillment of human spiritual values and needs. This is the endless task that is the permanent revolution, a continual development of the material and the spiritual.

Neither can socialism become a substitute for religion, a danger that is present when socialism is pursued mainly on the economic and material level. The rationality of science and technology cannot become the ideology of socialism, although there is the danger that it may be given such importance. In the socialist ideal, transcendence is surely not limited to material existence, with meaning in the world limited to the rational techniques of science. This would be a violation of the true socialist principle.[31] Socialist existence is conditionally in the world as it is also in recognition of the unconditional source of social existence.

Hence, the socialist principle incorporates both prophetic and rational expectation. "The tension between the prophetic and the rational elements in socialism is not a contradiction, but rather a genuine expression of a living expectation; it is that which constitutes its essence."[32] Our expectation is always transcendent and at the same time immanent. The prophetic goes beyond the known to a new creation; yet the rationality of expectation remains within the dimension of the knowable. Tillich states that expectation "looks for something 'other,' but not 'wholly other,' since that which is coming stands in direct continuity with what is present now."[33] The final expectation is a transformation of human nature and ultimately the revelation of the divine kingdom.

Socialism, theologically considered, then, looks beyond itself and its own achievement of a new social order. Tillich, near the conclusion of his discussion of religious socialism, makes clear that "socialism is not the end of socialism's striving," that the principle of socialism goes beyond concrete socialist forms in the creation of new being.[34] Marx would agree with this, and did in his own terms. The immanent expectation of socialism and the prophetic vision of the Judeo-Christian tradition are thus joined in symbol and in reality.

The socialist struggle in our age is a search for metaphysical meaning at the same time as it is a struggle for justice in human society. In overcoming human alienation and oppression, we come closer to knowing our true being. Capitalism, in its oppressions and alienating forms, has dulled the human spirit and all but killed the transcendent meaning of human social existence. In the struggle for a socialist existence, we hope to recover our wholeness, to heal the separation from the source of our being. Our prophetic hope is that the kingdom is near.

Social Transformation

Out of the final development of capitalism a socialist existence emerges. Capitalism is transformed into socialism when capitalism is no longer able to reconcile the conflicts between the existing mode of production and the relations of production, when the contradictions of capitalism reach a point where capitalism can no longer solve its own inherent problems. Capitalist relations become an obstacle to the further development of capitalism; new forms of production and social relations develop.[35] The forces within capitalist society, combined with the socialist alternative, create the conditions for moving beyond the contradictions of capitalism. Thus begins the transition to socialism.

The transition to socialism—in the concrete struggles of social existence—is the trend of history operating within

capitalist society. The transformation of capitalism to socialism comes out of the prior development of capitalism. Socialism is the dialectical abolition of capitalism. The development of socialism is, as Shlomo Avineri writes, "the realization of those hidden potentialities which could not have been
historically realized under the limiting conditions of capitalism." [36] Capitalism creates conditions and expectations that
it cannot satisfy; and since the potential cannot be realized
under capitalism, socialism becomes necessary.

The transition to socialism does not automatically or
completely dispense with the contradictions of capitalism.
Some bourgeois characteristics, such as market relationships,
"are inevitable under socialism for a long time, but they
constitute a standing danger to the system and unless strictly
hedged in and controlled will lead to degeneration and retro-
gression." [37] There is always the danger in transitional
societies that there will be retrogressions to former capitalist
relations. Within socialist society, as within capitalist society,
contradictions develop that require new adaptations. The
class struggle continues in the transition to socialism, and
beyond, to higher forms of social existence.

Each transition is a unique historical process that must be
understood as such. Nevertheless, all history is a continuous
transformation. Even with the overthrow of class domination, with the eventual transition to communism, the transformation of human nature and social order never ceases. The
disappearance of classes, the withering away of the state, the
elimination of the crippling forms of the division of labor,
the abolition of the distinctions between city and country
and between manual and mental labor—even with all these,
we are moved to a higher plane where other transformations
become possible. As one level of human and social development is reached, another becomes evident. Out of the seeds
of the past and present our future takes shape. We move from
one historical epoch to another.

Ultimately, social transformation involves and represents the creation of conditions to make possible a more just and meaningful social existence. By the construction of appropriate conditions we are able to realize the possibilities of our essential human social nature. Our lives now, rather than being determined by objective necessity, are lived with an emancipated consciousness. Social existence can now be developed with a transformed consciousness instead of consciousness being determined by the forces of circumstances.

Our history, in other words, is not independent of the material conditions of existence—the basic insight of historical materialism. This insight is theologically confirmed as well, indicating "that man lives on earth and not in heaven (or, in philosophical terms, that man lives within existence and not in the realm of essence)."[38] The human ability to create consciousness and to realize the spiritual qualities of being human depends on the conditions that allow for consciousness and spirituality. The creation of consciousness and spirituality, in turn, influences the development of material conditions. Material existence and spiritual existence—a spiritual existence that appeals to the transcendent character of the universe—are inseparable. Social transformation is a transformation in material conditions and a transformation in the way the sacred character of existence is integrated into daily life.

The material and spiritual reconstruction of social existence, to be known in our own age in the transformation to a socialist existence, means the emergence of a radically different type of sensibility. It is a sensibility, or a consciousness, that requires the integration of the sacred and the secular. No longer will existence be lived entirely within the secular and material realm of existence. Much more will be involved, namely, an existence willed with social and ultimate concerns. Capitalist existence, as "a form of human existence characterized by artificiality, selfishness, the inhuman and

dehumanizing pursuit of success measured in terms of pres-
tige and money, and the resignation of responsibility for the
world and for one's neighbor," will be replaced by the
struggle to realize a social existence that is prophetic in the
historical project.[39] An oppressive social existence, one that
is materially bound and inhuman even within the material
realm, is opposed in the struggle for a justice that is the
immediate and concrete demand of prophetic love. This is
embodied in the historical and contemporary struggles
against capitalist regimes, struggles that unite political action
and religious faith.

The creation of the good society—or, to use the Judeo-
Christian metaphor, the kingdom of God—is the objective of
the movement that brings together the sacred and the secular.
Social transformation is a historical event filled with transhistorical significance. Social existence and its continual
transformation now have significant meaning. Transformation and daily existence are meaningful because they are also
filled with metaphysical consideration. Symbolism is thus
restored to revolutionary life, giving infinite quality to
human life. The human situation, rather than completely
bound by time, is thereby elevated into the universal and the
transhistorical. Reconciliation—social transformation and the
becoming of social existence—is realized in an apprehension
of the eternal.

In social transformation the world is being revealed to us.
There is eschatological significance in the revolutionary practice of transforming the world, of creating a divinely inspired
justice and peace on earth. Our humanly conceived future
presupposes an assumption about the ultimate future.[40] The
struggle for a socialist existence is inspired by a metaphysic
on the ultimate purpose of human existence. We are witnessing an unfolding of the universal and divine reign in a coming
age of peace and righteousness.

The future of social existence, and our struggle for that existence, is thus guided by an eschatology of the ultimate future. The whole world in which we exist is understood on the basis of the future kingdom. This is the message—coming to us out of our Judeo-Christian heritage—that prompts us daily to the struggle for social existence.

The future is the good news. Our final expectation is for a new creation: "a radical transformation of human nature, and in the last instance—since human nature constantly grows out of nature as such—a transformation of nature and its laws."[41] Social existence and its transformation are redeemed through the grace of that which we understand as providence.

The task in the days ahead is to re-create the language and the symbols that will allow us to grasp and live more fully our existence. We desire to hear the word, to be called again.

Meaning in the World

In the creation of the symbols for our social existence, we attempt to come to terms with the ambiguity of the universe. The social existence that we construct and infuse with meaning is our collective human creation to deal with our presence in the universe. In our myths we try to apprehend the breaking of the eternal meaning into finite historical existence. Within history and time, as we know them, there is the kingdom. We search for the signs in our social existence that will reveal to us that which has unconditional meaning. In the end, however, in our social existence, the ambiguity remains ultimately.

The meaning of life is conditioned by our social existence; the meaning of life is in social existence by attending at the same time to an unconditioned meaning in the universe. Death—in our human existence—is the end of the conditioned

and centered existence. Death fragments life into the universe. Yet, in all of the ambiguity, the future of human social
being is prophetically realized in a new dimension. The social
meaning of our existence is of final consequence.

We are not forgotten in our social existence, as part of all
humanity, and we are not forgotten in eternity. Paul Tillich
reminds us in his sermon: "That we were known from eternity and will be remembered in eternity is the only certainty
that can save us from the horror of being forgotten forever.
We cannot be forgotten because we are known eternally,
beyond past and future."[42] We are known eternally; our
being is rooted in the ground of all being in the universe. The
atoms that make up all living and nonliving matter, including
ourselves alive and dead, were in the universe at the moment
of creation. All of us, all things in the universe, are grounded
in that first primordial atom of billions of years ago. Hence,
"nothing truly real is forgotten eternally, because everything
comes from eternity and goes to eternity. . . . Nothing in the
universe is unknown, nothing real is ultimately forgotten."[43]
The universe does not forget itself. The universe is in the
expanding process of knowing itself.

That we should speculate about the universe in order to
ground our social existence is the extension of all ambiguity.
The desire to know finally confronts firmly the reflective
project. We are now at the point in astronomical discovery
and the construction of concepts about the universe where
religion and science no longer have boundaries. In recent
decades the questions have emerged: What, if anything, came
before the beginning of the universe? Is there life of some
kind, including human life, on other planets in other galaxies? Will the universe expand forever? If and when the
light of the last star burns out, will the universe fade into
darkness and come to an end? Or will the universe cease to
expand, then contract until it gets so dense that there will be
another explosion and a new creation?

If we do not have a metaphysic and a symbolic system to live our social existence adequately, how can we begin to cope with these universal questions? And if we cannot cope with these questions, how can we begin to give ultimate meaning to our social existence? To avoid meaning is symbolically to hurl ourselves into the darkness of the cosmos. The mystery will remain. But our prophetically human goal is to find meaning in the world. This is our part in all beginning and ending—in creation and consummation.

NOTES

1. Paul Tillich, *Political Expectation* (New York: Harper & Row, 1971), p. 96.

2. Erich Fromm, *The Art of Loving* (New York: Harper & Row, 1956), p. 88.

3. James Luther Adams, "Theology and Modern Culture: Paul Tillich," in *On Being Human Religiously: Selected Essays on Religion and Society*, ed. with introducation by Max L. Stackhouse (Boston: Beacon Press, 1976), p. 235.

4. Paul Tillich, *Theology of Culture*, ed. Robert C. Kimball (New York: Oxford University Press, 1959), p. 133.

5. Paul Tillich, *Morality and Beyond* (New York: Harper & Row, 1963), p. 14.

6. *Ibid.*, p. 20.

7. Anthony Giddens, *New Rules of Sociological Method: A Positive Critique of Interpretative Sociologies* (New York: Basic Books, 1976), p. 44.

8. A. R. Louch, *Explanation and Human Action* (Berkeley: University of California Press, 1966), p. 235.

9. Terry Eagleton, *Criticism and Ideology: A Study in Marxist Literary Theory* (London: New Left, 1976), p. 187.

10. See Glenn Graber, "The Metaethics of Paul Tillich," *Journal of Religious Ethics*, 1 (Fall 1973), pp. 121-122.

11. Paul Tillich, *Systematic Theology*, Vol. 3 (Chicago: University of Chicago Press, 1963), p. 272.

12. Thomas Luckmann, *The Invisible Religion* (New York: Macmillan, 1967); J. Paul Williams, *What Americans Believe and How They Worship* (New York: Harper & Row, 1969); Andrew M. Greeley, *Religion in the Year 2000* (New York: Sheed & Ward, 1969); Charles Y. Glock and Robert N. Bellah (eds.), *The New Religious Consciousness* (Berkeley: University of California Press, 1976); Peter L. Berger, *A Rumor of Angels* (Garden City: Doubleday, 1970).

13. Christopher Lasch, *The Culture of Narcissism: American Life in an Age of Diminishing Expectations* (New York: Norton, 1978).

14. See Dietrich Bonhoeffer, *Ethics*, ed. Eberhard Bethge (New York: Macmillian, 1965). Bonhoeffer writes: "It is as whole men, as men who think and who act, that we are loved by God and reconciled with God in Christ. And it is as whole men, who think and who act, that we love God and our brothers" (p. 54).

15. Robert C. Neville, *Soldier, Sage, and Saint* (New York: Fordham University Press, 1978), p. 101.

16. *Ibid.*, p. 102.

17. See Roger Garaudy, *From Anathema to Dialogue*, trans. Luke O'Neill (New York: Herder & Herder, 1966), p. 39. Also see Russell Bradner Norris, *God, Marx, and the Future: Dialogue with Robert Garaudy* (Philadelphia: Fortress Press, 1974), pp. 1-14.

18. Herbert Aptheker, "Response," in Nicholas Piediscalzi and Robert G. Thobaben (eds.), *From Hope to Liberation: Towards a New Marxist-Christian Dialogue* (Philadelphia: Fortress Press, 1974), p. 52.

19. Paul Tillich, *The Protestant Era* (Chicago: University of Chicago Press, 1948), p. 258.

20. Rosemary Radford Ruether, *The Radical Kingdom: The Western Experience of Messianic Hope* (New York: Harper & Row, 1970), pp. 199-200.

21. Norris, *God, Marx, and the Future*, p. 39.

22. James Luther Adams, "Socialist Humanism and Religion: Karl Marx," in Stackhouse (ed.), *On Being Human Religiously*, p. 158.

23. Shepherd Bliss, "Latin America—Where the Dialogue Becomes Praxis," in Piediscalzi and Thobaben (eds.), *From Hope to Liberation*, p. 195.

24. Tillich, *Theology of Culture*, p. 42.

25. See John R. Strumme, "Introduction," in Paul Tillich, *The Socialist Decision*, trans. Franklin Sherman (New York: Harper & Row, 1977), p. xiii.

26. *Ibid.*, p. xx.

27. Tillich, *Socialist Decision*, p. 63.

28. Zygmunt Bauman, *Socialism: The Active Utopia* (New York: Holmes & Meier, 1976), p. 36.

29. Paul Ricoeur, *Political and Social Essays*, ed. David Stewart and Joseph Bien (Athens: Ohio University Press, 1974), p. 234.

30. *Ibid.*, p. 240.

31. Tillich, *Socialist Decision*, esp. pp. 80-82.

32. *Ibid.*, p. 112.

33. *Ibid.*, p. 110.

34. *Ibid.*, p. 132.

35. Karl Marx, *A Contribution to the Critique of Political Economy* (New York: International, 1970), pp. 19-23.

36. Shlomo Avineri, *The Social and Political Thought of Karl Marx* (London: Cambridge University Press, 1969), p. 150.

37. Paul M. Sweezy and Charles Bettelheim, *On the Transition to Socialism* (New York: Monthly Review Press, 1971), p. 27.

38. Paul Tillich, *On the Boundary: An Autobiographical Sketch* (New York: Scribner, 1966), p. 88.

39. José Miguez Bonino, *Christians and Marxists: The Mutual Challenge to Revolution* (Grand Rapids: Eerdmans, 1976), p. 31. Also see Hans Küng, *On Being a Christian*, trans. Edward Quinn (Garden City: Doubleday, 1976), pp. 25-88.

40. See Roy J. Enquist, "Utopia and the Search for a Godly Future," presented at the annual meeting of the American Academy of Religion, New York, November 1979. Also see Wolfhart Pannenberg, *Theology and the Kingdom of God* (Philadelphia: Westminster Press, 1976.

41. Tillich, *Socialist Decision*, p. 111.

42. Paul Tillich, "Forgetting and Being Forgotten," *The Eternal Now* (New York: Scribner, 1963), p. 34.

43. *Ibid.*, p. 35.

6

Nature of the World

What happens once you find yourself looking into the universe? All seems to become different and everyday life is no longer the same. We are part of an expanding universe; our galaxy is on a collision course with other galaxies; the ultimate fate of the universe is a mystery. What is the meaning of the cosmos and our brief moment within it? What is it that we are to do in the world?

Within the small realm of that which we practice as social science, new questions arise when we become universally conscious. If social science retains significance, it does so as a part of a greater awareness. We are traveling at great speed across the sky. We are on a journey. Human survival on planet Earth is endangered by our own endeavors. Are we directed by a purpose?

Our search is for a holistic vision in the social sciences. In these times our reflections and understandings are disjointed and ambiguous. At once we are coming apart and trying to put together a new sensibility. A new way of seeing is needed; a new way of speaking is to be found.

The Natural World

We all are on a pilgrimage, searching for meaning in the world. The human need is to understand life and death in

165

terms that transcend the self and the concrete events of social existence. Our present age is one of sacred void; there are few shared symbols that give meaning to our private and social existence. Often we are lost, adrift and battered by the elements around us. How are we to find the way? The larger meaning of our existence may be very near, within the nature of the world of which we are a part.

That we are part of the natural world is a starting point. Every particle, force, and organism in the universe is inter-related in a wholeness, a oneness in nature. And what we know as human life on this single planet is no less a part of that nature. That in our time we have separated our human being from nature can only be a brief departure from the manifest meaning of nature. In proper perspective, what is of interest in human nature is *nature* itself. The realization is as sobering as it is liberating. Our nature is revealed to us in the lines of the Swedish poet Pär Lagerkvist:

Some day you will be one of those who lived
  long ago.
The earth will remember you, just as it remembers the
  grass
and the forests, the rotting leaves.
Just as the soil remembers,
and just as the mountains remember the winds.
Your peace shall be as unending as that of the sea.[1]

The natural world, therefore, is no longer to be regarded as the *thing* "out there" that is manipulated and transcended by human beings. Rather, we are within the whole material world, participating in all that is and ever has been.[2] Wherever the universe originated and is going, there we are also. In a mystical sense, because of being enveloped in the universal process of creativity, we are traveling to eternity.

The natural world seeks a balanced wholeness of inter-related parts. The historically created human cultures of this earth have oriented themselves variously to the balance. Some cultures have violated the balance, spreading them-selves out unnecessarily and exploiting until they harm other ecosystems, as well as their own. They have become "bio-sphere cultures" that in the course of "development" destroy the balance of the world.[3] True development, on the other hand, is the creation of forms that advance and secure the interrelatedness of the natural world, including and enhanc-ing the human welfare as part of natural wholeness.

The philosophy of wholeness and the oneness of nature is an old one. The wholeness of the natural world is understood and celebrated in the sixth-century B.C. writings of Lao Tzu. An ethic of humility before nature—before ourselves and all else—is expressed in the lines of the *Tao Te Ching:*

> Surrender yourselves humbly: then you can be trusted
> to care for all things.
> Love the world as your own self; then you can
> truly care for all things.[4]

In our own Western tradition, only when we lose our lives in that which is larger do we find life. That something larger is in the world of nature, creating the natural world.

The wholeness of nature incorporates what we humans conventionally distinguish as the "supernatural." However, rather than a mystery existing apart from the natural, that mystery is firmly within all that is nature. The supernatural is natural, and the natural is at the same time supernatural. In the human search for meaning, the natural is not to be transcended; the transcendent is within the nature of the world. Such understanding departs from an anthropocentric humanism that places the human being apart from nature and

removed from the "supernatural" of nature. The meaning of
our being is within the mystery of the natural world.

We are provided with a theology, a theology of nature,
when we recognize the supernatural mystery of the natural
world. The secularization of the contemporary age has meant
not so much the demise of the sacred as it has meant the
infusion of the sacred into every realm. Now, since the sacred
is not a separate quality for particular realms, everything in
the world is touched with sacred meaning. Everything in the
world of nature—in the only world there is—is sanctified. All
of life has become wondrous and "religious." In traditional
terms, the whole earth and the universe of which it is a part
are of divine nature; all is related to God.[5] With the modern
recognition of the sanctity of the whole world, nothing
remains mundane and ordinary; everything is of transcendent
significance.

Yet in our contemporary civilization we continue to deny
the wholeness and the holiness of nature. The dominant
Western world view separates human beings from nature and
places them above nature, freeing the human species to
attempt a domination of nature. The consequence of this
view is the increasing disruption and destruction of the
natural environment, including harm to the human life that is
part of the environment. However, what is to be mastered in
our time is not nature per se, but *human nature*, by "bringing
under control the irrational and destructive aspects of human
desires."[6] Only when we fully apprehend our own place in
nature will we protect and preserve the environment of which
we are a part and in which we are nurtured and have the
possibility of being human.

The ecological relation of human life to the total environment is gradually coming into human consciousness. Environmental awareness is evident in various social realms, including
suggestions for a new ecological paradigm in the social
sciences.[7] Balance in the world of nature has been the theme

of the contemplative naturalist. Some time ago, Aldo
Leopold wrote the classic naturalist principle: "A thing is
right when it tends to preserve the integrity, stability and
beauty of the biotic community. It is wrong when it tends
otherwise."[8] This sense of balance and proportion—of the
love of nature—is necessary if the world, including human
life, is to survive.

Especially in the course of capitalist development over the
last century, the relation of the human species and human
social institutions to the natural world has been disrupted
and endangered. A just and humane society can only be one
that promotes the proper relation of human life to the rest of
the natural world.[9] The way we live in the natural world—the
way we structure our political economy—determines the
possibilities of our being human and our possibilities of
surviving as human beings. The *human* essence of nature is
that we as human beings become conscious of our place in
nature. This is the realization of the humanism of nature.

Nature and Community

The trend of Western capitalism has been increasingly to
exclude the naturalistic from all realms of life. Capitalist
development has relied upon and encouraged the domination
of nature.[10] The consequence is the dehumanizing of human
life and the denaturing of the rest of nature. A mode of social
relations exists that depends on the manipulation of human
beings, just as all else that is natural in the world is manipulated and exploited.

A critique of developing capitalism is thus a critique of the
exploitation of nature, as it is also a critique of the exploitation of human life. A social system that allows human life to
be harmed is one that lacks reverence for the entire natural
world. It is unlikely that human life can be considered fully

human unless it is included in a holistic vision of a spiritual-
ized naturalism. The development of a socialist society can
only be complete—can only be possible—if the alteration in
social relations and the underlying mode of production is
according to a naturalist vision of the world. Otherwise, a
truly human transformation in social relations is impossible.
Any transformation without a basic naturalist ethic would
create the same horrors that characterize capitalism.

We are clearly in a dark time. Human survival and progress
toward a better world can no longer be taken for granted.
The optimism of our conventional Western wisdom is wearing
thin. A new sensibility is gradually emerging, one in which
"we must learn either to think in the dark or to think darkly
if we are to integrate consciously what is already our experience."[11] A depth of understanding is required that allows us
to apprehend the problematic survival of that aspect of
nature that takes place on this earth. A naturalism of
humanity—a synthesis of nature and community—is the
depth of understanding that is needed in these dark times.

That our time may be running out is the message of recent
prophetic scholarship. Documentation on the scarcity and
further destruction of natural resources, the depletion of
energy supplies, the perpetuation of dangerous political and
military systems, and the general deterioration of the human
condition is contained in recent works.[12] If the transition to
a new age is not made with a grace that takes naturalism as its
source, human extinction and the extinction of much else
that is of nature are likely to be certain. The human being
could well go the way of other vanishing species.

The destruction of our existing civilization might easily
come with nuclear war. Given the destructive technology of a
deformed political process and a deformed culture, E. P.
Thompson warns, a nuclear holocaust is probable within the
next thirty years. The threat occurs in a "Satanic Kingdom,"
in a world where "repressed violence has backed up and

worked its way into the economy, the polity, the ideology and the culture of the opposing powers."[13] The menace of nuclear war reaches far back into the national development of the great powers, producing forces that direct us to the military use of nuclear weapons. Whether these forces can be turned back requires "nothing less than a world wide spiritual revulsion against the Satanic Kingdom."[14] Turning back the destructive forces similarly requires, I am arguing, an infusion of naturalistic reverence of the world into human imagination and into the deep structures of political and economic reality. The world can be saved only with a respect for the essence of that world, all that is of nature.

What is needed, if our survival is to be assured, is a fundamental change in our conception of nature. A conception that respects the sanctity of all that exists, has ever existed, and ever will exist is a naturalist conception that allows for the necessary transformation in the political and economic structures of the world. To be surpassed in a new attitude toward the world is the widespread feeling of meaningless that characterizes the contemporary age. The search for meaning, as Viktor Frankl terms it, is not to be fulfilled by further destruction of our being, but by a conception that exalts our being as a natural part of the universe.[15] Meaning and survival are to be found in the spiritual and natural dimension of existence.

What is to emerge is no less than a metaphysic for our time. Our postsecular age is coming to an end, or must come to an end, if the natural world of which we are a part is to continue and if we are to give a humane meaning to our existence. The naturalist metaphysic infuses into our everyday experiences a universal meaning, a meaning that places everything within a context of natural wholeness. This is a metaphysic that finally transcends the traditional religious symbols. Rather than assuming a dualism of this world and the "other" world, the naturalist metaphysic gives meaning to all that exists and to what the world may become. The whole universe is of sacred and spiritual significance.

The human being in the human community becomes a "caretaker" in the world.[16] Caretaking is within the human sphere, as it is in the care of all of nature. As nature's caretaker, the human community is sensitive to the intrinsic needs of nature and to the natural requirements of human existence. The naturalist metaphysic provides the whole world with meaning and places the human community in a position of responsibility for the transformation and survival of the world.

The naturalist metaphysic views everything as a part of the web of life. The human being, as the most hightly developed, toolmaking animal, "must recognize that the unknown evolutionary destinies of other forms are to be respected, and act as a gentle steward of the earth's community of being."[17] This is a metaphysic embodying the love of nature: "Balance, harmony, humility, growth which is a mutual growth with Redwood and Quail; to be a good member of the great community of living creatures."[18] The respect for all life provides hope for the preservation and growth of human life.

The naturalist metaphysic, in departing from a theism of the duality of separate existences, is a profoundly religious outlook. Sacredness does not reside only in a particular Supreme Being; rather, all of the universe is filled with meaning. All of existence is, in the words of Nathan Scott, a *sacramental universe.*[19] Hence, our radical faith is that all of existence, all of nature, is steadfast and deserves our trust. There is in the world that which is transcendent of every particular being, yet present in every being. All is thereby holy, a truly sacramental universe, an expression of divine grace. The naturalist metaphysic is a return to a vision of the world as a sacred reality.

Faith in nature signifies our coming home, finally finding a place in the world. It is finding what was there all the time. We search for human community and for a oneness with the world. To come to the revelation that we are part of the natural world—that we have a place in the scheme of things— is to find that we are at home in the world. With the homecoming that is ours through nature, we recognize our place in the human community.

The search for a home in the world is the ultimate human struggle. That a home is not often readily and concretely available to us is the problem of an underdeveloped human sensibility and an oppressive social structure. The commitment of a life to one place in the world is penalized in a social economy that stresses the geographical mobility of its people. Yet the natural human need is for the stability of place. There is the effective bond between people and place, a bond secured by fellow human beings, by the physical landscape, by the everyday reality of the place of which we are part.[20] The philosophy of place is an old one, yet we are found wandering: "Do you believe there is some place that will make the soul less thirsty?"[21] In a naturalist metaphysic we learn to stand firm. What is of nature is already in the place, at home.

In our time the tension remains between the search for a human community and the attachment to nature. We tend continually to separate the human and the human in social relations from the world of nature. In a better world, one that is both humane and natural, the human community and nature are joined in holistic union. The human community is part of the natural world, and the world of nature is known in human terms. We have found a place in the world of nature when the human community has become naturalized, when nature has become humanized.

Nature and Transcendence

Within nature is that which we have been seeking all along—the transcendent. In our Judeo-Christain tradition we have tended to remove the godhead from the world of nature, nevertheless remaining uneasy about the particular presence of God within the natural world. Other religious traditions, the Eastern religions and Native American traditions especially, as well as the "primitive" religions, have dealt in a more inclusive way with the religious character of that which is about us and of which we are an integral part. The end of the Christian era, which we are probably witnessing, comes with the incorporation of nature into new religious symbols.

The modern situation, it seems apparent, demands the continuous involvement of life in the reality of the physical universe, rather than attempting to experience another reality, complete and perfect, apart from the natural world.[22] The transformation of religious sensibility nevertheless retains the absolute condition of transcendence. There remains the unconditionality of the universe—of nature—that gives meaning to all experience. Still demanded in the modern situation is a faith in the beneficence of the universe. Still required, as required always, is a faith in that which is unknowable. In transcendence there is always something beyond, a something that gives ultimate meaning to our existence.

This is transcendence which insists that "no finite person or object or community is ultimate but is rather integral to an encompassing reality that alone is worthy of final trust and loyalty."[23] The finite continues to be apprehended in the infinite, but the infinite is a reality that encompasses the whole universe in the dynamics of its development. The transcendent is *within* the world, not an entity separate from the universe. Transcendence includes all that is, and the unity of all that is is in the universe. This is a transcendence that follows from increasing ranges of contemporary thought and experience. Theologically, George Rupp notes, "propositions about a transcendent personal being who intervenes on request in nature and history are not compelling even to many who nominally subscribe to them."[24] A naturalist metaphysic offers the symbols for our emerging religious sensibility.

Transcendence is of unconditional character in the natural world, rather than an attribute of an entity "outside" the world. The notion of transcendence, as Robert Bellah has observed, is retained in our search for a contemporary religious sensibility.[25] Transcendence is the necessary symbolic process that allows us as individuals and as a society to grasp reality as a whole. We are thus permitted to make sense of our experiences and to give direction to our actions. Emerging from our historical experiences, the symbols that recognize transcendence refer to the totality of being, linking concrete events and experiences to the whole of experience. There is meaning in the universe.

The transcendence of self is a natural human requirement. As Frankl notes, "When the self-transcendence of existence is denied, existence itself is distorted."[26] Our being is reduced to a mere thing, an object, when being is not related to the whole of experience in the world. To be whole as human beings, we necessarily reach beyond our selves and our species. We become human only as we become a part of the whole universe.

Paradoxically, it seems that the truly religious nature of self-transcendence is recognized in the experience of solitude. In solitude, before nature, the self is denied. For Thomas Merton, the Trappist monk, the inner self discovered in the desert is not an isolated self but a self immersed in all of nature and humankind.[27] In the "transcendent experience" the self ceases to be aware of itself as a distinct subject. Merton writes: "To attain this experience is to penetrate the reality of all that is, to grasp the meaning of one's own existence, to find one's true place in the scheme of things, to relate perfectly to all that is in a relation of identity and love."[28] No longer conscious of ourselves, in such transcendence, we experience a oneness in the universe. Existing everywhere, we are no longer ourselves.

The true self, then, is the self that is immersed in the totality of the universe. This is the self that has "lost" itself, a self that finds itself only in emptying itself into the wholeness of the world. In the New Testament there is divine reconciliation when the self rediscovers its union in the totality of God.[29] In the purity of love, everything is united and everything is pleasing to God.

The self-transcendence that is present in the natural world likewise allows the union of the human being with the totality of the natural universe. As we become lost, immersed, in the world of nature, we regain the original union. For Henry David Thoreau, being lost in a wood was a memorable and valuable experience. Only when lost, "turned round," do we appreciate the wonder of nature. "Not till we are lost," wrote Thoreau, "not till we have lost the world, do we begin to find ourselves, and realize where we are and the infinite extent of our relations."[30] Going beyond ourselves, outside of ourselves, and in loss of ourselves, we begin to find our place in the world.

Finding ourselves through transcendence, as a naturalist metaphysic indicates, does not necessarily entail a theism of the divine. In fact, the naturalist ontology explicitly attempts to frame the question of the transcendent in other than theistic terms. Beyond theism is a symbolism that dispenses with the classical duality of subject and object. That which is of divine character is not necessarily, as Carl Raschke observes, "an object that can be represented and manipulated in accordance with the structures of the experiencing subject."[31] A reconstructed metaphysic goes beyond the subject-object dualism in which human beings are the subjective arbitors of an anthropomorphic Supreme Being.

The "postmodern" theme, with considerable variation, conceives of the world as a sacramental reality rather than the province of a supernatural being.[32] Assumed is an essential wholeness and coherence of the world. The naturalist metaphysic, as I am calling it, finds the divine everywhere, in everything. A pantheism of the pervasiveness of the divine in nature may be tempered by a philosophical "panentheism" that simultaneously envisions the divine beyond all.[33] Whatever the variant of the naturalist metaphysic, however, the divine is to be found in the midst of the world, not removed from this world in another world.

In this way, as the process philosophical perspective suggests, the divine is at the same time both the totality of the world and the actual entity that is the totality.[34] There is divine *immanence* in the world while there is also divine *transcendence*. According to the naturalist metaphysic, the world of nature—the whole of the universe—has the quality of being equally immanent and transcendent. The mystery and the wonder of nature, what we call the "divine," is an integral part of the world, touching every part of the world, giving a transcendent meaning to every part. The world has a wholeness touched by mystery—all from within the process of its own creation and development.

The nature of the world is that of movement and change within the whole of the universe. The naturalist metaphysic conceives of the divine world as an evolving primordial reality. This is a total vision of the world, a vision, as Thomas Altizer reminds us, that is essentially Oriental.[35] Contrary to the Christian tradition, or perhaps to be absorbed into that tradition, is the vision of the totality of the world, of the world as the Totality or All. Because the divine is in the world and embodies the world, the primordial reality is the All. The unfolding of the world, then, is the consummation of the Totality.

Our human religious conception of the world is likewise in a process of movement toward possible fulfillment. Nature, as the totality of created things, is conceived in human terms with great historical variation. Yet, in the religious sense, we all apprehend the divinity of the natural world through inwardness, or as Paul Holmer phrases it, "the nearness of God is determined by the quality of the heart, mind and will."[36] As I have been indicating, the substance of that which we experience as God or the divine is moving from an earlier dualism of the two worlds of reality to a contemporary holistic vision of the creation and evolution of the universe. In the new vision—the naturalist metaphysic—the divine is in the totality of the world. The mystery of nature is present from the beginning, and the human course, as it is part of the development of the universe, is to find a harmony with all other parts of the world. We live and we die to become closer to the world.

The current movement in the human world is toward the construction of "new structures of existence."[37] There is the possibility of creating structures that will bring us into closer harmony with the wholeness of the world. On the other hand, it is just as likely that the human species may become separated from the necessary interrelatedness and balance of the world, destroying the natural environment that makes human life possible. An evolving naturalist sensibility, one of religious proportion, offers hope for the course of human survival. That we may find the Way is the prospect offered in a holistic vision of the world. This is a vision that must come to inform our labors as social scientists if our work is to be for human survival rather than destruction. We must realize our part in the nature of the world.

The Way of Nature

The way of our work is the way of nature. As we come to live in harmony with the nature of the world, we become

part of the true reality of existence. Our world then has
meaning and significance and plays its part in the true order
of things, in the natural development of the universe. Reverence for the world and our part in it becomes a central
concept of the emerging human sensibility, a sensibility that
also furnishes a foundation for that which we do as social
scientists. A new *naturalism* provides us with holistic vision
and an ethic in the social sciences.

Naturalism, as the way of nature and the way of our
production, begins by recognizing the mystery that appears
in all of nature. Mystery, contrary to the positivist mode,
inheres in and is indispensable to our existence in the
world.[38] It touches all parts of the natural world and ultimately fills all things with a meaning that is beyond explanation. The mystery is sometimes apprehended only poetically,
as in James Wright's concluding lines in "Milkweed":

Whatever I wept for
Was a wild, gentle thing, the small dark eyes
Loving me in secret.
It is here. At the touch of my hand,
The air fills with delicate creatures
From the other world.[39]

And as Galway Kinnell closes in a poem, alluding to that part
of us that is in the mystery of nature:

But I know I live half alive in the world,
I know half my life belongs to the wild darkness.[40]

Recognizing the mystery of nature *and* our nature as
human beings, we are partly in the darkness of the universe.
Loren Eiseley has written that "we have come from the dark
wood of the past, and our bodies carry the scars and un-
healed wounds of that transition."[41] He notes that we are
haunted by the "night terrors" that arise from the subter-

ranean domain of our collective development. "Not for nothing," Eiseley adds, "did Santayana once contend that life is a movement from the forgotten into the unexpected."[42] In that mystery we are both lost and found in nature. Inhabiting a spiritual twilight on this planet, we cannot but experience the mystery. In a poetic sense, we humans flow transparently through the nature of the world.

In our time there is the problem of language, of how we are to grasp the mystery of the natural reality of the world. Poetry has the abstractness and the symbolic power that often allows us to break through our everyday language barrier, allowing us to grasp fleetingly the mysterious reality of nature. The linguistic problem is evident in our contemporary inability to capture the universal meaning that traditionally has been found in the language of a godhead. The mystery of the universe has been conveyed to us in the identity of God, providing us with the deepest and most ultimate source of meaning. However, as Altizer observes, "We have surely entered a world, and above all a language world, in which there is not only the absence of all names or images of God, but more deeply absent the very possibility of naming or identifying God as God."[43] If we are to regain our place in the world, we must do so through the creation of a language that permits us to enter into the mystery of the universe. I am suggesting that the language is to be found in naturalism, in the way of nature. In nature we find a new presence and new identity of what we once named as God.

We are thus entering into a new narrative world as we enter the world of nature. As with all ventures into a new world, through language, metaphor, and the narrative we are in the process of redescribing reality.[44] It is as if the world becomes transformed. To use another image, we come to regain that which was lost in another way of telling the story. We are moving, it seems to me, to the very center of universal meaning—to the way of nature.

To what end is the world of nature, inquired Ralph Waldo Emerson, and how are we humans related to this nature? In his famous essay on nature, Emerson conveyed the sense of the divine that is close at hand in the natural world. "In the woods" he wrote, "we return to reason and faith." Continuing:

> There I feel that nothing can befall me in life—no disgrace, no calamity (leaving me my eyes), which nature cannot repair. Standing on the bare ground—my head bathed by the blithe air, and uplifted into infinite space—all mean egotism vanishes. I become a transparent eyeball; I am nothing: I see all; the currents of the Universal Being circulate through me: I am part or particle of God.[45]

Every natural fact, for Emerson, is a symbol of some spiritual fact. Nature gives us the necessary connection to that which is of universal meaning. We know from nature but, in the mystery of nature, "we know more from nature than we can at will communicate."[46] This is the unconditional grounding of reality in nature.

At the same time, and in the same woods, Thoreau searched for universal meaning in the world in nature. Describing his intentions of living for a period in the solitude of nature, Thoreau wrote: "I went to the woods because I wished to live deliberately, to front only the essential facts of life, and see if I could not learn what it had to teach, and not, when I came to die, discover that I had not lived."[47] Completing his "experiment" after experiencing all of the seasons, Thoreau observed that he had met "with a success unexpected in common hours," and that through such experience "new, universal, and more liberal laws" are established around one, and one comes to "live with the license of a higher order of beings."[48] A life immersed in the wisdom of nature provides a foundation for a truly meaningful human existence.

The nature essay—steeped in the experiencing of nature—is one of our contemporary forms of metaphysical reflection. The world of nature as seen through the reflective mind opens to us a new awakening. Nature is the text; the essayist, the theologian who reads the text and suggests the hidden and wondrous meanings that are buried within it. Reflecting upon our life in nature, we ask once again: Who are we, for what purpose are we here, and where are we going? The naturalist helps us, as Eiseley notes, to learn from the symbolism that is inherent in the nature that is around us and of which we are a part.[49] It is within the dark world of nature that we seek to know about our existence and the end to which we are being hurled.

So we have come finally to the pilgrimage, driven by the desire for satisfactions that are not supplied by the world as currently known. Life is a journey into the unknown.[50] Although the infinite realms of mystery remain, characterizing the essence of the world, we seek a form that will permit us once again to know a meaning in the world. Our true home, I am suggesting, is found only as pilgrims in the search for our home in the world. That world is in the world of nature. In our brief time the way of nature is also to be found in our practice of social science.

We are of an ancient form of endeavor, on the watch for a word, a sanctified meaning, an act of revelation. We are among, as Eiseley calls them, the chresmologues, "dealers in crumbling parchment and uncertain prophecy."[51] Our profession demands that we "be alert to signs and portents in both the natural and human worlds—events or sayings that others might regard as trivial but to which the gods may have entrusted momentary meaning, pertinence, or power."[52] The capacity is for recollection of our place in the development of the universe and the search for transcendent meaning of the future that has not yet appeared. The aim is for ever-increasing accessibility to the reality of nature. We are constantly trying to make ourselves ready by the simplist and most ultimate of means.

By a kind of life—in reflective contemplation—we humans come to an understanding about the nature of the world. Not by apparition but in the practice of our lives do we come to know. "It is a quality of habitude," the poet and observer of the natural world Kenneth Rexroth writes, "the result of a kind of life, of innumerable acts done."[53] The spiritual life of each of us is simply the life of all others and all else being made manifest within us. In the Dead Sea Scrolls, the question was raised by the Teacher:

> I that am molded of clay,
>   what am I?
> I that am kneaded with water
>   what is my worth?[54]

The world is in and through us. The unity of life is realized in natural and worldly responsibility.

In a life of contemplative and active naturalism, we accept nature as origin and ground, as the all-embracing totality. All of life as proper form is prophecy in which the mystery of the universe becomes a reality in everyday life. In the realm of social science the holistic vision of naturalism furnishes us with a prophetic mode of understanding and acting.[55] We are concerned with the future of the human community, a community and future that cannot be separated from the destiny of the world. Our form of address calls human beings to an awareness of their natural and historical responsibility. The critical objective is to promote that which will assure the survival of the natural world and to be a part of the struggle in transforming our own human history. Only in a vision that embraces the nature of the world will our prophetic hope be made possible.

NOTES

1. Pär Lagerkvist, *Evening Land*, trans. W. H. Auden and Leif Sjoberg (Detroit: Wayne State University Press, 1975), p. 49.
2. See Paul E. Lutz and H. Paul Santmire, *Ecological Renewal* (Philadelphia: Fortress Press, 1972), pp. 93-97.
3. Gary Snyder, *The Old Ways* (San Francisco: City Lights, 1977), pp. 57-66.
4. Lao Tzu, *Tao Te Ching*, trans. Gia-Fu Fong and Jane English (New York: Random House, 1972), p. 13.
5. Frederick Elder, *Crisis in Eden: A Religious Study of Man and Environment* (Nashville: Abingdon Press, 1970), pp. 81-128.
6. William Leiss, *The Domination of Nature* (Boston: Beacon Press, 1974), p. 193.
7. William R. Catton, Jr., and Riley E. Dunlap, "A New Ecological Paradigm for Post-Exuberant Sociology," *American Behavioral Scientist*, 24 (September/October 1980), pp. 15-47.
8. Aldo Leopold, *A Sand County Almanac* (New York: Oxford University Press, 1966), p. 240.
9. See Karl Marx and Friedrich Engels, *Marx and Engels on Ecology*, ed. Howard L. Parsons (Westport: Greenwood Press, 1977); Sebastiano Timpanaro, *On Materialism*, trans. Lawrence Garner (London: New Left, 1980).
10. Leiss, *Domination of Nature*, pp. 178-190.
11. Charles E. Winquist, "The Subversion and Transcendence of the Subject," *Journal of the American Academy of Religion*, 48 (March 1980), p. 59.
12. Richard J. Barnet, *The Lean Years: Politics in the Age of Scarcity* (New York: Simon & Schuster, 1980); William H. McNeill, *The Human Condition: An Ecological and Historical View* (Princeton: Princeton University Press, 1980); Jeremy Rifkin with Ted Howard, *Entropy: A New World View* (New York: Viking, 1980).
13. E. P. Thompson, "A Letter to America," *The Nation* 323 (January 24, 1981), p. 89.

14. *Ibid.*, p. 93.

15. Viktor E. Frankl, *Man's Search for Meaning: An Introduction to Logotherapy* (New York: Simon & Schuster, 1963), pp. 151-213.

16. H. Paul Santmire, *Brother Earth: Nature, God and Ecology in Time of Crisis* (New York: Thomas Nelson, 1970), pp. 149-153.

17. Gary Snyder, *Turtle Island* (New York: New Directions, 1974), p. 91.

18. *Ibid.*, p. 97.

19. Nathan A. Scott, Jr., *The Wild Prayer of Longing: Poetry and the Sacred* (New Haven: Yale University Press, 1971), pp. 43-75.

20. See Yi-Fu Tuan, *Topophilia: A Study of Environmental Perception, Attitudes, and Values* (Englewood Cliffs: Prentice-Hall, 1974).

21. Robert Bly, *The Kabir Book: Forty-Four of the Ecstatic Poems of Kabir* (Boston: Beacon Press, 1977), p. 17.

22. George Rupp, *Beyond Existentialism and Zen: Religion in a Pluralistic World* (New York: Oxford University Press, 1979), pp. 34-37.

23. *Ibid.*, p. 105.

24. *Ibid.*, p. 197.

25. Robert N. Bellah, *Beyond Belief: Essays on Religion in a Post-Traditional World* (New York: Harper & Row, 1970), pp. 196-207.

26. Viktor E. Frankl, *The Unheard Cry for Meaning: Psychotherapy and Humanism* (New York: Simon & Schuster, 1978), p. 53.

27. Thomas Merton, *Seeds of Contemplation* (New York: Dell, 1960), pp. 3-24.

28. *Ibid.*, p. 31.

29. See Dietrich Bonhoeffer, *Ethics* (New York: Macmillan, 1965), pp. 17-63.

30. Henry D. Thoreau, *Walden,* ed. J. Lyndon Shanley (Princeton: Princeton University Press, 1973), p. 171.

31. Carl A. Raschke, "The End of Theology," *Journal of the American Academy of Religion,* 46 (June 1978), p. 170.

32. See Scott, *The Wild Prayer of Longing,* pp. 52-60.

33. See Charles Hartshorne and William L. Reese, *Philosophers Speak of God* (Chicago: University of Chicago Press, 1953).

34. See Robert B. Mellert, *What Is Process Theology?* (New York: Paulist Press, 1975), pp. 58-63.

35. Thomas J.J. Altizer, *The Descent into Hell: A Study of the Radical Reversal of the Christian Consciousness* (Philadelphia: Lippincott, 1970), pp. 173-183.

36. Paul L. Holmer, *The Grammar of Faith* (New York: Harper & Row, 1978), p. 211.

37. Robert C. Neville, *Creativity and God: A Challenge to Process Theology* (New York: Seabury Press, 1980), p. 120.

38. Karl Rahner, *Foundations of Christian Faith: An Introduction to the Idea of Christianity*, trans. William V. Dych (New York: Seabury Press, 1978), pp. 44-89.

39. James Wright, "Milkweed," in *The Branch Will Not Break* (Middletown, CT: Wesleyan University Press, 1963).

40. Galway Kinnell, "Middle of the Way," in *Flower Herding on Mount Monadnock* (Boston: Houghton Mifflin, 1964).

41. Loren Eiseley, *The Star Thrower* (New York: Harcourt Brace Jovanovich, 1978), pp. 53-54.

42. *Ibid.*, p. 54.

43. Thomas J.J. Altizer, *Total Presence: The Language of Jesus and the Language of Today* (New York: Seabury Press, 1980), p. 27.

44. See David Tracy, "Metaphor and Religion: The Test Case of Christian Texts," *Critical Inquiry*, 5 (Autumn 1978), pp. 91-106; Hayden White, "The Value of Narrativity in the Representation of Reality," *Critical Inquiry*, 7 (Autumn 1980), pp. 5-27.

45. Ralph Waldo Emerson, *Selected Writings of Ralph Waldo Emerson*, ed. William H. Gilman (New York: New American Library, 1965), p. 189.

46. *Ibid.*, p. 200.

47. Thoreau, *Walden*, p. 90.

48. *Ibid.*, pp. 323-324.

49. Loren Eiseley, *The Night Country* (New York: Scriber, 1971), pp. 143-149.

50. See Elena Malits, *The Solitary Explorer: Thomas Merton's Transforming Journey* (New York: Harper & Row, 1980), pp. 21-52.

51. Eiseley, *Night Country*, p. 62.

52. *Ibid.*

53. Kenneth Rexroth, *An Autobiographical Novel* (Garden City: Doubleday, 1966), p. 399.

54. Quoted in a poem, "Take Care of the Kit Fox," by Loren Eiseley, *The Innocent Assassins* (New York: Scribner, 1973), p. 97.

55. See Richard Quinney, *Providence: The Reconstruction of Social and Moral Order* (New York: Longman, 1980), pp. 102-115.

Index

About the Author

RICHARD QUINNEY is the author of numerous works on the problems and contradictions of contemporary society. His previous books include *The Social Reality of Crime; Critique of Legal Order; Class, State, and Crime; Capitalist Society;* and *Providence: The Reconstruction of Social and Moral Order.* Born in rural Wisconsin in 1934, he received a Ph.D. in sociology from the University of Wisconsin, and has taught in universities on the East Coast. He and his family live in Providence.